Praise for

notes from A Grunt Lawyer in the Trenches

"Solid, hard-hitting review of the legal profession. Succinct recollections of a life spent guarding a unique trust in society and our Constitution. This is a must-read for everyone in the legal profession – trust me, they need it." **Cdr. KIRK S. LIPPOLD**, USN (Ret) – Commanding Officer Destroyer USS COLE; Author of Front Burner, Al Qaeda's Attack on the USS Cole; Fox News and CNN Contributor.

…,"notes from A Grunt Lawyer in the Trenches" is appreciated more than I can state. Read it, know it, spread it, and demand some accountability from a government gone batshit crazy. **TED NUGENT**, Rock Star; Author of Ted, White & Blue.

'Grunt Lawyer in the Trenches' is a gem of a read. I kept thinking; "Wow, I wish I had read this before my tango with the justice system!" I hadn't even finished the introduction and had collected several shiny pearls--Councilor Rob informs the reader about how things really work for 99% of us seeking justice, all with a keen eye, mind and wit wrapped in a genuinely compassionate heart. Rob skillfully shares case-stories that reveal truths about the justice system--the lawyers, the clients, the judges, the police, the process--the wisdom and pearls he has collected over his well-heeled career passed to us--Truly brilliant and downright fun to read--you will laugh and gain rare insights from a master grunt lawyer in the trenches. **PAMELA J. LUNA**, DrPH, MST

notes from

A GRUNT LAWYER IN THE TRENCHES

Forty Years in The System
California & Wyoming

Robert J. DiLorenzo
Attorney at Law

DEDICATION

This book is dedicated to all court personnel, including court clerks, research clerks, Judge's Assistant's, Bailiffs, who make it all work - and to all other grunt lawyers who have dedicated their lives to this calling, without regard to whether they got paid or not.

To those who are in this profession for the money, fame, and notoriety - I refer you to Michael Avenatti, now housed within New York's Metropolitan Correctional Center.

TABLE OF CONTENTS

Introduction

INTRODUCTION

Sinking Down into The Trenches

Choosing a career as a sole practice trial lawyer can be a bitter-sweet life choice. I say, "life choice" and not "career choice" because choosing the law as a career is indeed a life choice, more than you can possibly imagine. It will affect every aspect of your life from your relationship with your family and friends, to how people relate to your choice of what you do for a living. You will no longer see your community or human nature the same way. In the converse, people, your friends, and family will never see you the same way, either. You will be admired, but oftentimes reviled. Your life will never be the same. If you are the type that must be liked by everyone, choose a different career. You will be happier for it.

I have been a lawyer for over 40 years in both California and Wyoming, concentrating on criminal law, civil litigation, and family law problems. What has made my practice so unique is that I have seen the law operate from two diverse perspectives on life, morals, social and political beliefs. There are no two states so different in so many ways. I have handled

i

cases in the big cosmopolitan cities, in the suburbs, small towns of California, and the rural areas of Wyoming where the population of cows and pronghorn far exceeded the number of people. In large part, I never spent much time litigating oil and gas law, environmental law, constitutional law (other than Fourth and Fifth Amendment issues), corporate or securities law, nor was I a Supreme Court appellate lawyer who practiced in the United States Supreme Court, to present an argument on an obscure constitutional or federal regulatory provision. Those high-brow specialties, or concentrations, are reserved for what Justice Neil Gorsuch called the "perfumed lawyers." Those are the guys or gals with the Armani or Brooks Brother's suits.

My specialty or concentration, if you can call it that, was down and dirty courtroom law, the getting your hands dirty, kind of law. Lawyers of my ilk are in the trenches up to our necks, and sometimes those trenches are deep, muddy, and nasty. When I use the word 'grunt,' I respectfully borrow the word from its more common meaning to describe the U.S. Marines, the down and dirty combat soldiers that always seem to go in first, that take on all comers who want to take what is ours, that is, our property, and our freedom. Some of us lawyers are the grunts who do the kind of law most regular working-class people seem to get involved in and are familiar with. This is the law most genteel lawyers are neither familiar with nor would stoop to lower themselves to deal with. We wear suits from Macy's, Land's End or JC Penny's. Unless you are a Public Defender, then it's corduroy and Born shoes. Not the most profitable kind of law but can be the most rewarding. We are the grunts who protect the property and the lives of those with no power from those with power who want to take it. Some cases are sad, incredibly sad. People can and will do bad, and sometimes stupid, things. Some are just downright funny. I seem to have spent years, most times unwittingly, amusing more courts and judges than I can count. In any case, I know few grunt lawyers who are in it for the money. In many cases there is none. What you will come away with is a career worth celebrating, and a life worth living.

Every time I see a lawyer movie, I usually end up laughing through it, or shaking my head. The movie stars playing trial lawyers constantly show the glamour, the I gotcha, the dazzling oratory, the stunned silence, the screaming "I want the truth!!!" moments. Trust me, those moments are few and far between. Being a grunt sole practitioner is a time consuming, drudge endeavor. Forget the 40 hour a week gig. Not going to happen. Your social life, whatever you had left after law school, will suffer. Being an average litigating grunt lawyer can be the most personally rewarding, sometimes profitable, yet, most annoying, upsetting, amusing, financially disabling, shocking, embarrassing, depressing, and downright most stressful profession you can choose. You will lose sleep, and lots of it.

Most of the cases described here were settled without trial, as are the great bulk of cases that come before the courts. You do not go to trial if the State has you on the ropes. You do not go to trial when the stop and detention is good, within constitutional bounds, and you have no chance of excluding the incriminating evidence, the confession, etc. You do not go to trial when the chances are slim to none to prevail, and the client tells you he did it. The time comes when you must have a long talk with your client and tell him he needs a "come to Jesus' moment." Similarly, civil trials are usually settled since neither party has any desire to throw the dice whether it be by jury or by the Court.

In criminal cases, many of my clients come to see me when they are angry and upset. Sure, they are angry. They had been arrested, not a happy experience. They were denied their freedom, even for a relatively short period of time, whether it by a warrant or caught in the act. They were handcuffed, placed in the back seat of a police cruiser, sent to jail, booked, mug shot taken, fingerprints taken, subjected to a blood alcohol test, etc. They were placed in a jail cell with other model citizens, so, of course they are pissed and angry. Some are remorseful. "I can't believe I drank as much as I did." Or "I can't believe I was so stupid." And, as is usually the case, they were arrested on a Friday and kept until their first court appearance on Monday. Please take note, the police love to serve warrants on Friday, and will go out of their way to do so. They love to keep you locked up until Monday, your first court appearance.

On Monday comes their initial appearance. This is where the judge advises the entire happy audience. He advises them of their Constitutional rights. That includes all those in custody in gauche orange fabrics, and those who were lucky enough to be given only citations. The Court will always emphasize that they have a right to an attorney whether they can afford one or not. The Court will call each case and ask them how they wish to plead. Of course, the plea is "Not Guilty" until such time as the case is investigated, or until the defendant secures counsel. If the accusation is a felony the defendant will not be asked to plea but be informed of his right to a preliminary hearing to determine the probability of his committing the crime described in the police officer's affidavit. The Judge will then determine the bail to be set, the amount, and whether it be cash, bond, or signature. The Court will ask questions as to whether the defendant can afford a lawyer, and, if not, a lawyer will be appointed to represent each defendant if they come within certain income limits. Those appointed lawyers are the Public Defenders. In many cities these lawyers are overworked and underpaid. They do the best they can under the circumstances.

Usually, it is the family that gives me the call on a Saturday or Sunday. That's right, defense attorneys never have a day off. People have problems seven days a week. You either go see the client immediately or see him first thing in the morning.

You must ask the client the usual questions such as his employment, years within the community, family in the area, prior convictions, if any, whatever can affect the court's assessment of flight risk. You must do what you can to get this person out of jail, and deal with the bail amount, the flight risk issue, whether to get it lowered or secure a bail bond, signature bond, or OR (own recognizance) release. On one occasion I was retained by a family to represent a young man. I appeared in court and found the young man had green hair. Do you know what a man looks like with green hair and wearing an orange jump suit? Yes, that's right. The court room chuckles were inevitable. Since then, every time the prosecutor referred to my client, he called him "Mr. Carrot."

Some states, including New York and California, have become "no bail States." This concept of no bail is relatively new, and I have no experience with it, since Wyoming is not one of those states. Some reform may be needed, since a few prosecutors I know use bail as a form of punishment without trial or a determination of guilt or innocence, to those who cannot afford bail. At the same time, however, it seems to me that a "get out of jail free card" given to even low-level violent offenders may translate to a "catch and release" program, which has not worked well with Immigration and Customs Enforcement, since few ever show up for court. It is common sense that a no bail program will not work well without a risk assessment in place. The system must trust the judges to make an assessment as to the defendant's past criminal history, the possibility of re-offending, of harassing the victim or witnesses, nature of the offense and its seriousness, and so on. Not just defendant's rights, but protecting the public, has got to be paramount in the mind of judges. Our forebears knew this a thousand years ago when they instituted laws and the police to enforce them in order to protect the innocent from inevitable predators. Have no illusions, it's rough out there.

Typically, after their happy experience in Court, they see you again, but at the office, where they tell you "The cops are picking on me!!" How many times have I heard that! Of course, after your fourth violation of probation, they are still picking on you! Most of my clients manage not to re-offend, some do. Some just take longer to learn the facts of life. Some never do. Unfortunately, I have seen it all too often over the years. It is the inevitable phrase, "I did something stupid."

What many of these clients do not realize is that the police are smart and know who is doing the bad things. They know. They arrest you, see you in the courts, in the jails, and they know that if they see you on the streets, especially in small towns, they know they have at least a 50/50 chance of an easy bust. All they need to do is get a good stop and detention. And they usually do. The suspect will invariably fail to make a complete stop or fail to signal a turn, which gives the police a legal basis, or probable cause, for the stop. Then they have you. In some cases, overly enthusiastic officers will overreach. In one case I had, the officer stopped my client biker because he believed his handlebars were too high! (I got that case dismissed). Often, the officer may smell marijuana emanating from an open car window, or find the driver is intoxicated from whatever, or the driver may have had contraband in plain sight on the seat, or an occupant may have an outstanding warrant. It's a short trip to the county jail.

Most lawyers I know do not ask the client as to his or her guilt. They simply do not want to know. They will defend based on the evidence they have and nothing more is said. I have never done that and will never do that. Yes, I ask them outright: "did you, do it?" "If you say "no" then be prepared to convince me. Because, if you cannot convince me, then how will you or I convince a jury?" Sure, I can, and have been criticized for my approach by colleagues, but I am the one who must live with my decisions and look at myself in the mirror when I shave. Face it, the recidivism rate is way too high and repeat business is a way of life for us. You don't want to put that client back on the street where you know they will harm someone else or themselves, yet again. Every lawyer knows that or should. That is not to say my clients are not vigorously defended. They are, and I will file and argue any motion be it motion to dismiss, or motion to exclude evidence if my client's constitutional rights were violated. After all, that is what we do. We grunt lawyers are the most effective and sometimes only bulwark against governmental tyranny.

I have seen too many lawyers take most all cases to trial no matter what, without looking for an alternative outcome that might just help the client, and the community he lives in. Lawyers make far more money taking matters to trial rather than seeking alternatives. Lawyers know that too. For clients that can afford to pay the fees, the time spent in litigation is money in the bank. Even a low-level felony will cost upwards of $20,000 to try a case. We all get paid by the hour. It doesn't take much to rack up the time for court appearances, motions, research, interviewing witnesses, conducting discovery, interviewing experts, preparation for trial and the days spent in trial. Lawyer's love to go to trial. It's what we do. We love to listen to ourselves. Besides, the lawyer goes home every night even if the client does not. Ask Harvey Weinstein.

Yes, even the Public Defenders have their nutty lawyers as well. I knew a Deputy Public Defender, who just happened to be the sibling of a Hollywood film maker, who took on every case as a "cause" against the "racist, capitalist legal system". The Deputy demanded that every case go to trial, no matter what the client had done, no matter what the evidence proves, and no matter how many priors the client had. No plea bargains, no wheeling, no dealing, no lecture with clients. The deputy just apparently transferred full responsibility of the Defendant's actions onto the community and the system at large. The lawyer made a big to do about it all with the media. They care more about their political views, and their virtue signaling, than they do their clients. These lawyers may feel good about their morally superior opinions of "social justice," but you will be the one doing the time. What really annoyed me about this Deputy was that it made life exceedingly difficult for the Chief Public Defender of the county. This was a good man doing the best he could, given the situation of too many clients, not enough time, not enough courts, and not enough money. He retired soon thereafter.

Clients in civil cases such as personal injury (PI) matters are different, yet quite similar. In PI cases, the clients are also angry. Someone did them an injustice. Their rights had been violated by someone doing something they were not supposed to do. Or they were injured by the fault of someone else. When you are a young pretty female and a passenger in a vehicle driven by an incipient, dim-witted teenage boy, trying to impress his friends with the new Mustang mom and dad bought him, and he crashes the car causing grievous injuries, your life changes. Or interview a client whose neighbor violated his deeded easement or interfered with his water rights. Clients who do not get along with their neighbors can be particularly challenging. These clients seem to take everything on a personal level when someone interferes with their property in some way. These people are always upset, if not downright angry. It is all too close to home, literally. They want what they believe belongs to them, and they want it now, and the other guy can go to hell.

Personal injury lawyers are ghouls. I admit it, I'm one of them. We can put a price on the loss of every appendage, can calculate the price on every possible injury, from every possible incident to every possible person, no matter what the age, gender, or pre-existing condition, whatever. We can take a simple rear end automobile crash at 15 miles per hour that results in a whip lash or neck sprain and make it appear as a major life changing event in which the plaintiff will never again be able to enjoy life, be able to hug their grandchildren, or even place them on their lap.

In these civil cases, a lawyer must make sure the clients are properly compensated for their injuries, loss of employment, pain, suffering, and any future problems. This can be an overly sensitive matter. It is not only the individual client that is involved here, but the family as well. Their loved one has been injured by the fault of another and they are not happy people. In most of these cases, the lawyer gets involved with his most natural of enemies, and that is insurance companies. When liability is established, most companies will do the right thing and compensate for the injuries, and quite often it is policy limits. Some insurance companies take quite a bit more work. And some, well... You get the picture. There are insurance companies that always play hard to get. They do it even when liability is clear and established. These companies want a reputation for being difficult, lest they be taken advantage of. They will use any excuse for not fully compensating your client, challenging every medical billing, and estimates of future pain and suffering. You will earn your fee.

Clients in child custody divorce matters are not just angry, they are incensed, filled with rage. For them It's win at all costs, and all else be damned. The clients in many of these family law cases become irrational. All the emotions are on display here. Jealousy, envy, love, hate, wrath, rage, revenge, will rear their ugly head in these cases. Just wait until your client is told by you that he must pay spousal support and give up half his retirement to a woman he now detests, has been unfaithful, and has spent the last fourteen years consuming every penny he had earned in income on herself. Marriage may be expensive, but nowhere near as expensive as divorce.

The most difficult are the child custody problems. The way our system operates there is no way to insulate the children from those emotions in the raw. And this is where the system fails those children big time. In all my years as a lawyer I have never had my life threatened in a criminal case. But in family law matters, my life had been threatened three times! In one incident, an opposing party saw me in his rear-view mirror on a street, stopped his car, got out and threatened to kick the crap out of me. Lucky for me a cop car pulled up and carted him away. Not one of the happy times being a lawyer. That's what I get for doing my job. Look, family law is not for the faint hearted, the overly sensitive, the thin skinned. Most lawyers will stay far, far away from it.

Clients are few that are completely happy with the result of any divorce or child custody matter and that is because when the courts make the decision - no one is happy. Who feels comfortable putting their family's future in the hands of a stranger in a black robe? Clients are in effect suing themselves. The longer the case continues without a settlement, the more expensive it becomes, for both parties. The spouses are in effect depleting the marital estate. I have seen cases where when the clients got through fighting each other there was nothing left to distribute. Shear foolishness.

When children are involved, judges are in the position of splitting the baby, playing King Solomon. This is one of the areas of law in which litigation should be discouraged or curbed. Mediation and settlement are the only way to handle these cases. It should always be about the children. The kids are always caught in the middle of it all. No matter how much your clients tell you they do not involve the children, they are involved. They talk to the children constantly, trying to get them to his or her side, trying to get the kids to tell the court they want to stay with mom or dad. They try to buy the kids gifts or promises of more freedom, or anything else they can think of. Sometimes the animosity between the parents is so great the children feel every ounce of that rage and are torn between the parents with no way out.

In one incident, it was well known within the courthouse that these two parents were fighting tooth and nail over their son. This 13-year-old boy was the object of repeated court appearances in which the parents could not even make a basic agreement on anything. These two were in court on an almost weekly basis. The two lawyers should have known better but were doing simply what their clients wanted - to fight. One morning, at the law and motion calendar, we lawyers were all waiting for the hearings to begin. The judge walked to his bench in a somber yet angry mood. He started by showing us a large photograph of this 13-year-old boy, the son of the parents we were discussing here. The boy had the night before committed suicide by putting a gun to his head. The pressure on the boy was just too much for him to bear. The judge was angry, and lectured all the lawyers present that this tragedy is what happens when the lawyers forget the children and merely play to win at all costs.

This incident affected me deeply. I never again handled family law cases the same way. I will go out of my way to settle these matters. I repeatedly ask the Court that these cases be subject to mediation and many times opposing lawyers fight me on this. They do not want to lose their income. I know this for a fact. I have seen it far too often. Some courts have county supported mediators who do their best to resolve the differences between parents. They succeed most of the time. Mediation is the best way to handle these matters, period. The courts are simply unequipped to do a good job and to create a peaceful and functional environment for these kids.

In a case I handled recently, the mother would not allow her 9-year-old son to visit with his father and would not under any circumstances. I represented the father and we tried everything to convince opposing counsel and his client to permit visitation. No dice. The mother used as an excuse "the boy has autism, and the father doesn't understand autism." We filed an action, and then endured months of the Discovery process in which they wanted everything from this poor father. The dad was a simple ranch hand on a large cattle ranch in Montana making $2,500 per month. Yet they wanted detailed tax returns, employment records, work schedules, telephone records, banking records, checkbook registers, you name it they wanted it. This is a simple man who just wanted to see his son on a regular basis. The court ordered an investigation, and it was found the usual: the father loves his son and is deserving of visitation. Still no visitation. The father goes to counseling sessions on autism. Still, no visitation. I ask the Court for mediation. The mother doesn't show up. We try again. She shows up, no visitation, the mediator, a retired judge gives up on her. I repeatedly tell opposing counsel that the court will give this man visitation and that he should know this. I mean the statutes are centered around family values, family stability, the fundamental and substantial rights of parents, and most important of all, the best interests of the child. Opposing counsel withdraws from the case. New opposing counsel substitutes in. We then start all over again! He wants new Discovery, new payroll records, new phone records, the same tax returns, on and on. I know what is happening here. They are trying to exhaust the man, both in patience and money. I got fed up with the case since it had been going on for nearly two years! It goes to trial. What happens? The Court gives the man his rightful custody and visitation on a regular schedule! Tens of thousands of dollars in attorney's fees were spent on this case that could have been spent on the child. But no. It got so expensive for my client that I had to forgive many thousands of dollars in fees. But what the hell, it was for a good cause.

The case illustrates the weakness in the judicial system. These cases do not belong in the trial courts. It only makes the problem far worse. Mediation must be mandatory in every matter that involves children. The mediator should make a recommendation or report to the court as to the progress of the case and the issues involved. There are times when it is proper and even preferential that a judge lectures the parties and convinces them of their responsibilities as parents to work together for the sake of the children. But no, it does not work that way in many states, especially Wyoming. It is as if the lawyer lobby will not condone this change since their incomes might be affected, in the negative. How are the "best interests of the child" advanced by litigation? I would certainly like to know. I have seen far too many families crippled by the pain of litigation. It makes the parents even more antagonistic to each other and that does no one any good at all.

Most litigating lawyers hate family law and wouldn't touch it. The stress is too high, the rewards too little, and the loss of sleep too great. I knew one lawyer friend who was retained by a man to reduce the spousal support he was paying the ex-wife. He found she had a new job, and he believed the support level should be lowered. The lawyer files the appropriate motion for a support modification and goes to court. Because the support level had not been reviewed for a time, the court reassessed the entire support level and raised the sum to be paid to the ex-wife. My lawyer friend was incensed over this, got a bloody nose, and never again took on a family law case. Sometimes it is better to leave well enough alone.

Expect your "life choice" to affect your relationship with your family and friends. At one time or another someone in your family will get into trouble. So, who are they going to call? You guessed it. You're the man. There you are at a family gathering, and she starts in on you as to what someone did to her or what situation she has found herself involved in. You are family, of course, you want to help. But be aware. These situations can get very thorny at times. Representing a family member leaves you open to the very thing a good lawyer is not supposed to be, and that is subjective. A good lawyer must be objective, but only appear to be subjective, and yet see the matter for what it really is, without the fog of emotions. You must tell the client/relative the hard, cold truth of it all. For some, that can be quite impossible. Your relationship will never be the same.

Of course, they expect you to do all this pro bono, for free. That can be very troublesome. Having a family member as a client can be an awful experience. It can affect your income in a most negative way. Look, the only thing you must sell is your time and your expertise. That is how we make a living. When you are spending a great deal of time correcting the wrongs of a family member, you are not concentrating on your clients, and your income will suffer. There are so many hours in a day, for billing purposes. Your debts will have to wait. I know of many lawyers who do not take any family causes for just that reason. Some will take them but will bill lightly. As a distant cousin lawyer would say: "look, you need a lawyer. You might as well pay me rather than a stranger." But, in any case it will be a no-win situation for you. No matter what happens, whether you go to trial or not, or settle the matter or not, they will never be completely happy, you will get the blame, be held responsible for the outcome. No good deed will go unpunished.

Most people view lawyers in a negative light and much of that negativity is well deserved. In our civil and criminal justice system, lawyers are enormously powerful people. They know how it all works when most people do not. They are adept at getting what they want and using the system to full advantage, even in their own personal lives. The public, on the other hand, often see lawyers on TV and in the media, as they sometimes grate and prey on society, and take up causes that are unpopular in the extreme. These lawyers become addicted to the attention, become media hookers who must be the center of attention. Many of them will have their day in the spotlight, use a client or two for their own selfish purposes, then when the State Bar or the law finally catches up to them, they fizzle, are disbarred, or sent to prison. Ask Michael Avenatti.

Yes, many lawyers are good people. They have integrity and will never make irrational, specious arguments to the court or will ever use the system to gain an unfair advantage. Many lawyers do care about their clients. Most lawyers I have dealt with are of this quality. Then there are the soulless lawyers. These people will do anything to gain advantage. These are the lawyers who believe that winning is everything, and that anything you can do to win, whether it is honest or not, is fair game. These lawyers only care about themselves. The problem with these lawyers is that they attract the most heinous, narcissistic, sociopathic people as clients, who will do and argue anything in order to win. I have seen way too many of these lawyers. I know this from experience. Stay away from these lawyers. Unless of course, you are a heinous, narcissistic, sociopathic person.

When I see friends or acquaintances in public places, be it restaurants, saloons or on the streets, they ask, "hey Rob, how ya' doin?" I respond, "Just trying to earn an honest living." "Honest living!?" That's when they start to laugh, never knew one who didn't. Sure, they laugh. Negativity as to lawyers has been around for hundreds of years. It is ingrained in our culture. It was Shakespeare who said, in his play "Henry VI, "First thing we do, let's kill all the lawyers." Is there anyone out there who has not heard a lawyer joke? Much of the negative public's perception is also fueled by the media, movies, and the high-profile cases you see on TV news, as well as the public's personal experiences with lawyers. I must admit, in America, a dislike of lawyers is almost ingrained. In colonial Massachusetts in the early 1700's there was a shortage of lawyers. A letter went out to London. Could they "send over a few honest attorneys, if such a thing existed in nature?"

Much of the perception is fueled by the legal community itself. People ask me repeatedly why I would try to defend and set free a client I knew to be guilty and dangerous, or to put on the stand a client I knew would lie to save himself. The answer is simple. I have never purposely done such a thing in 40 years of practice. I have never defended a client I thought was guilty of the crime charged and dangerous to himself and others, in order that he walked free without any consequences. I have never placed a client on the stand knowing he would lie his butt off. In those rare incidences where I have taken advantage of police error it was done because the Bar states that I must or be disciplined, suspended or worse. Lucky for me most have not city been truly bad guys, but clients who have made errors in judgment.

Insofar as the popularity of lawyers, or lack thereof, one telling incident comes to mind. One year, in North-Eastern California, I produced a sanctioned rodeo. We decided at the intermission, we would have as entertainment a "Bull-Poker" event. This event was very popular in rodeos. How the game goes is a card table is set up in the middle of the arena, 4 cowboys sit at the card table acting like they are playing poker, then let the bulls out. The last cowboy sitting at the card table wins the cash. Of course, a bunch of cowboys dared me to sign up for the event with the old standby, "are you afraid?" After a few beers, I stupidly volunteered to sit at that card table. On the day of the event, the rodeo announcer went from cowboy to cowboy asking their name, occupation, etc. "Oh my, what am I going to say?" The announcer knew very well who I was. Not thinking of anything else, I blurted out "I'm a lawyer." The crowd laughed. They then let out these big, fat, healthy bulls into the arena. Two of the cowboys ran like hell. Cowards. I and this young cowboy refused to leave. My pride was at stake.

At that point, the entire crowd of hundreds of people just instinctively, without any direction at all, began to yell and stamp their feet in unison: "GET THE LAWYER!" "GET THE LAWYER!" In fact, the rodeo clown stood behind me waving his arms over his head at the bulls! The crowd was laughing and cheering him on. The crowd certainly would not have shouted that sort of epithet if I were a plumber! "Get the plumber!" just does not sound quite right. Sure enough, the bull, like a locomotive, ran through the card table at me, and tossed me in the air! That bull zeroed in on me a second time but missed. The crowd was happy, but at my expense! I was incredibly lucky, all I had were black and blue bruises. As a footnote, the rodeo was televised locally, wherein one of the county judges saw the whole thing while relaxing at home with a brandy and questioned me as to my sanity come Monday morning at a pre-trial conference. However, I did win the cash.

Many people dislike lawyers because we set criminals free and "get them off on legal technicalities." Contrary to popular belief, dismissals based on "legal technicalities" are quite few and far between, having experienced only a few. In one matter, my client was arrested for a misdemeanor crime but was not specifically charged for nearly three years. When I received the case, I thought the case was far too stale. I could not find any rational reason why the case had been delayed for so long. As citizens we have a constitutional right to a speedy trial. Pre-charge delay often prejudices the defendant, big time. Witnesses move away, can no longer be found, or memories fade. I filed a motion to dismiss based on prosecutorial delay. At the hearing, the court analyzed the reasons for the delay. The court found intentional procrastination, and an overcrowded docket as weighing against the prosecution. The court also found that my client also "got lost in the system." The prejudice against the defendant was too great. The case was dismissed. It is our constitutional rights that protect us all from an overpowering system. As lawyers, it is our obligation to protect us all from that sort of abuse.

Money is another issue altogether. Money and lawyers have become a parlor joke, thinking all lawyers are wealthy. That is certainly not the case. I sometimes tell friends and saloon buddies that in my practice "you're innocent until proven broke." You get a big laugh at that one. Private lawyers are expensive, sure they are. When you are paying $300 per hour for a lawyer you better get results. When I started out in this profession, I charged $75 per hour. As my experience increased so did my fee. $300 may seem a great deal of money and for some, it is. However, what you are paying for is experience, knowledge of the system, and knowing just what a court will do in a given situation. That kind of knowledge only comes with a great deal of experience which is repeated by yet another client.

A law school professor once told me to "get the money up front while the tears are still flowing." Good advice, but sometimes that cannot happen all the time. Frequently, the client simply can't come up with all the money up front. Half the time, I must take monthly payments. It all depends on the client, whether you believe he is honest and trustworthy or whether he is scamming you, which does happen on occasion. In one case, I sympathized with this married couple with a neighbor problem and only took a small retainer. They said they would pay me on a regular basis. I did a complete trial for three days for them and won everything for my clients in that real estate easement case. I was rewarded by receiving a letter from the bankruptcy court informing me that I was named as a creditor by my client! Despite repeated promises, I was paid nothing!

Understand that $300 per hour is small change compared to the fees charged by big city attorneys. There, it is double, even triple my fee. These high-priced lawyers are the elite in the profession. These are the guys from Harvard and Yale that demand and get a starting salary of $200,000 or $250,000 per year. And if you were a Supreme Court clerk you get a bonus of another $250,000! That's a great deal of money for young lawyers, with no practical experience and still in their twenties! We grunt lawyers who do all the unattractive hard work in the filthy trenches dealing with course and indelicate common problems get a small fraction of that, and that is if the client pays you.

In today's practice of law, expect not to get paid in many of your cases. On many occasions, you will do the job your client expects, and still, you do not get paid. The lawyer is about that last bill the client pays on the ladder of priorities. In some cases, the State Bar has become their tool for avoiding payment on their bill. They will threaten to file a complaint with the State Bar against you for any imaginable reason or no reason at all, just to compel you to simply go away. Many lawyers do go away. There is nothing more nerve wracking or causing loss of sleep than fighting a complaint with the State Bar. Trust me, I know. I have defended lawyers before the State Bar. In all my years, I have been able to keep a clean record in both State Bars. If you are falsely accused by a client and the money is owed, don't cower in a corner, fight it. I have and will never shy away from services professionally performed and monies rightfully earned. The State Bars are just starting to come to grips with this problem of false complaints. But in the meantime, it stinks.

Quite often the client makes the matter far more expensive than it should be. You tell them the facts of life and they don't like it. Because the client is angry, they will constantly press you to ask for things that are inconsequential or irrelevant, or they will refuse to do the things that I know the court will want them to do. Many refuse to look at the big picture. Emotions and the law are a bad mix. So, you spend numerous hours doing what they ask or convincing them to do certain things and they then complain about the bill. You must tell the client what is possible and what is not and be firm about it. I know lawyers who are too emotional about clients or "causes." I know lawyers who have gone broke and left the practice of law because they have not bridled their emotions on the picking and choosing of clients, and their issues.

Clients come in all shapes, sizes, and attitudes. They run the gamut from the good, to the bad, to the ugly. Good clients are easy to get along with and advise. They hang on to your every word and take your advice seriously. They do exactly what is requested of them and even go out of their way to get you what you need to help with their case. But some clients find it difficult to just cooperate with their lawyer. For example, in a civil case, when you receive a proper discovery request for documents that the client has in his possession, and, after repeated requests by you to send them, and the client refuses, then you have problems. Some just refuse, telling you "It's none of their business," or whatever. Instead of trusting your judgment, the client must be convinced that the discovery request is proper and relevant to the issues before the court. After repeated requests to send the documents, with the repeated refusals, you must spend additional time to seek an extension of time from the opposing attorney to honor the request, beyond the 30- day due date. This ends up taking a great deal of time, with additional charges for your client.

Then there is the client who needs constant reinforcement. This is not a situation in which a lawyer fails to communicate with their client, which, I must admit, does sometimes happen. That should never be the case. What I am talking about is the client who wants to communicate on a near daily basis. You explain everything to them, but it is never enough. They constantly call for information about their lawsuit or their criminal matter. They call and ask the same question you answered the week before. These are the "hand holders." This is when a good paralegal or legal secretary becomes all important. It is a lot cheaper for a client to speak to a secretary than to a lawyer who charges by the hour. If the client continually wishes to speak to the lawyer about inane matters, then you must bill them for it. You would be shocked how the calls taper off after the client receives their bill.

Sometimes you will get a bad client with "serial problems." She retains you for a criminal case in a certain county. She pays you for that case. You get her released from jail. You then find out she has an outstanding warrant in a neighboring county for a different case you didn't know about, and she didn't tell you. She was arrested again in the neighboring county. You feel compelled to represent her in that case as well, since it may affect the outcome in the case you were retained in. You get her released again. Then you find out that because of these two cases, her ex-husband has refused to bring her daughter back to her home because of her criminal behavior. She calls you crying and wants you to represent her in a custody/visitation case! But all you have is the original retainer from the original single case you had accepted to take! This is not a fictitious scenario. Over the years, these types of "serial problems" have happened on several occasions to several different people. These are the headache cases, the cases in which you are sorry you took.

There are times when a client comes to you with a serious problem and no way to pay for it. This has happened to me numerous times. I either take the case alone or ask another lawyer to partner with me to share the work. Look, the profession has been good to me, and the least you can do is to occasionally take on these matters. If all lawyers did this, especially the large firms, we would all be better off, and, who knows, it might even improve our reputation.

Combat veterans with problems are in a different situation. I let it be known that I will consult with any such veteran for no charge. Sometimes their problems are serious, and sometimes they just need some advice. If the problem is serious, we charge only half my hourly fee. I must say, it is the least we could for these veterans who have given their all.

However, when lawyers constantly take on crusades for a client to do the right thing whether they get paid or not, it is their families that suffer. I respect lawyers that sometimes take these cases and have done so myself on many occasions. However, this Man Of La Mancha behavior can get you into real trouble. You cannot do this on a regular basis. The clients will leave you broke. In my years, I have learned to toughen up and not take each case as a "cause." You must learn to pick and choose your fights. I know a lawyer who went belly up, folded up his practice, because of too many pro bono cases. As for money, I could tell you this, if every client paid the bill, they received for my services over the past 39 years I would then be rich. Sometimes, you do let it go. But I want that to be my decision, not theirs.

My goal has always been to correct the problem the client is confronted with. You do the client no favors by giving him a get-out of jail free card or put him back on the streets in the same condition he was in before. That means the client, and the community, no good at all. Quite often, the problem is the client himself. Sometimes the client is in way over his head with addiction or some other mental or emotional problems that need to be confronted. What I have always tried to do is to fix the problem so the client can live a normal and healthy life and not be a threat to anyone, including himself. I know that sounds like we lawyers should also be a bunch of social workers. But lawyers have to be many things to many people. When that works, it's great! When it does not, it stinks. But it works more than you think.

Then there is the ugly client. This is the client that no matter what you do, no matter how successful you are with his matter he is not happy. He will argue with you over everything. He didn't like what you said to the judge, he is discourteous to your office people, he leaves nasty messages on your phone, he constantly complains about his billing, and is relentless by calling you every day for yet another problem that was developed by his not taking your counsel. My only advice in this situation is to just let them go. It does not take much to prepare and file a Motion to Withdraw. It will save you much needless anxiety, frustration, and loss of sleep.

Clients will make or break your practice. If happy, they will invariably refer a friend or a relative to take their problem to you. One good thing will usually lead to another, and another, and another. That is how we gain and preserve a good reputation for solving problems.

A litigating lawyer must have a strong stomach and be able to absorb a great deal of punishment, especially from other lawyers. Court rooms are battlefields, never think otherwise. Most lawyers on those battlefields are armed and dangerous. My first run in with an opponent was when I was a certified law student back in the 1970's, employed by the United States Attorney's Office in San Diego. I was assigned to go to Federal Court, for an arraignment. My opponent was a lawyer from the Federal Defender's Office. What a horse's butt he was. Before the hearing he sought me out, knowing I was very new, and began to rip me a new one, calling me names, castigating me with "who the hell do you think you are," doing all he could to put me down and put me off balance. As stunned as I was over it, when my case was called, I simply informed the court that I would amend the information and add an additional count on the shit head's client. He was not happy. But I was.

In big cases, when there is a lot of money at stake, or when the crime charged is serious, or in all family law matters, you must be prepared for the opponent that will cause you grief. Some will try to bully their way around you, call you names, try to rattle you. You cannot let them do that. You are forced to give it back to them. But always, always be civil, if you can. Sometimes civility is just not possible. I had a civil case back in the mid-eighties, against a county, in which the issue was whether the road was a county road or not. I'll be damned when I find that the opposing lawyer removed all references of that road from the County Supervisors minutes from the official records! There were pages missing! At a deposition, that issue came up and we had a pushing match. My secretary had to call the police!

In another incident, in Wyoming, I sued a bank for their failure to give an elderly employee her retirement. I had received my Bar card two years before. My opposing counsel was a partner in a large firm in one of our "cities." I know he, like so many others, looked up my name in the State Bar Directory and noticed I was admitted in 2007. He had no idea I have practiced in California since 1981. When we first met it was at a Deposition of my client. Thinking I was a new lawyer, he began to harass and insult me and my client. I immediately put a stop to that with a "who the hell do you think you are dealing with here. I don't tolerate this nonsense and never have in the 29 years of practice both in California and will not here." The case settled in two weeks. A good litigator cannot put up with pushy, arrogant lawyers. If they detect any weakness at all, they will try to eat you alive.

Being a trial lawyer requires a great deal of public speaking. You had damn well been good at it or at least feel comfortable speaking before a crowd of people. There are some lawyers that cannot speak or perform adequately in a public setting. As smart as they are, they cannot seem to perform and speak clearly in front of a courtroom. Lawyers know who they are. These are paper lawyers. They are particularly good at preparing briefs, researching the law, and finding all sorts of precedents in support of their issue. They have wonderful grammar and prose. But when it comes time to tell it all to the court, they fall flat.

I was co-counsel in a large, complex suit in which, at an important hearing, my co-counsel gave every indication that he was in panic mode. Just prior to the hearing, he was pacing, sweat was seen on his brow, and so on. When he did speak, he started to stutter, voice breaking, obviously appearing extremely nervous. This is when animal instinct happens. Your opponent picks up on that and goes in for the kill. However, I did most of the talking at that hearing, and had the all-important closing argument which, by the way, ended very well. For some reason, I do not get the jitters before court and have always remembered what was told to me by a trial practice teacher: just think of a judge sitting on a toilet with his pants around his ankles. Since then, I have always felt comfortable in court rooms. When my client informed the co-counsel to please let me do the talking in court from there on out, co-counsel literally started to tear up, close to crying. I was amazed and appalled, both at the same time. As for my co-counsel, always remember, Dirty Harry's sage advice, "a man has got to know his limitations."

This book is not a high-brow legal analysis of controversial cases or an in-depth look at the great cases and causes of our time. If you want that type of read, go to Justice Neil Gorsuch's most excellent book "A Republic If You Can Keep It." Most of those lawyers are "paper lawyers." They sit behind a desk all day, and formulate contracts of all types and kinds, prepare wills, trusts, deal with real estate problems, mediation of disputes, legal research for other lawyers, etc. Most lawyers are of this type. If that is what excites you, this book is not for you. This book is more in line with "The Troubled, If You Can Save & Redirect Them." My attitude towards litigation, the law, the courts, and the justice system, whether it be civil or criminal, has always been shaped by my background and some would say "unique" life experiences. One could say I am into conflict, since I have seen so much of it. But I have always had a heart for people and their problems and their all-too-often impossible situations. Helping people has always been job one. My life, both as a child and an adult, has shaped this attitude. Sometimes I have succeeded and sometimes I have not. Quite often the facts in any given case are not the whole picture. In most cases, the facts are only the beginning. I honestly believe that the most productive, problem-solving lawyers come not from privileged or silver-spoon backgrounds but from a past riddled with adversity, hardship, and struggle. These lawyers always deal with reality, in the way things are. As they say on the streets: "it is what it is." How else can you relate to the clients you are charged with representing and speaking for in court? Let me give you some background.

1
South Brooklyn and Beyond

I was born and raised in an inner-city culture. South Brooklyn was a great place to grow up in the fifties and sixties. It wasn't as fashionable back then as it is today. So, if you are reading this book and you want the full experience, please use a slight New York-Brooklyn accent since even after all these years away from Brooklyn, I still have that give away "he's not from around here" overtone.

Growing up in the Bensonhurst and Canarsie sections of Brooklyn was a far better educational experience than any college class I, or you, could ever take. You learn early to never go to a park at night. Never do or wear anything that makes you stand out from the crowd or attract attention. When walking in the city, always know who or what is in front of you, behind you, on your right or your left. Stay away from crowded tight spaces on subways, and always stand near the door. You never know when you need to make a quick escape. Never have a victim mind set. You would be asking for trouble. If need be, put on a tough guy attitude. Trust me, the bullies will leave you alone, even if you're shorter than average. In New York, we all knew it was the small guys with crazy eyes you had to fear. I know this from experience.

1

Now that we have the basics down, growing up was fun. Whether we played stick ball in the streets, ringo-levio, handball at the park, putting up thread cobwebs on sidewalks at night on Halloween, your first BB gun at Christmas. What we did not have in playthings, we made them. We made carpet guns (ask an old timer what that is), snow forts, big boxes as ships, you name it we did it or made it. We had fun. We played with anyone in the neighborhood, be they White, Black, Catholic, Jewish, Protestant, whatever. Unlike adults, kids are not particular on who they play with. Life was more predictable and simpler back then. You knew what was expected of you. We all had stable families, one mother, one father, a sister or brother. Nobody was confused as to their gender, wondering whether they were really males or really females. None of us were, or even thought we were, racial, ethnic, class, gender, homophobic, Islamophobic, transphobic, sexist, misogynist, whorephobic, microaggresive, or religious "victims." We all knew being and acting the "victim" was the death nell growing up in Brooklyn. It could get you punched or worse. We all knew Brooklyn could be a dangerous place and we planned and acted accordingly. Mayor Giuliani came later.

I went to public schools. Not a great experience. Did well in grade school, lost interest in junior high and rarely went to high school. This was the age of busing. Sure, a new high school was only a few blocks from the house, but the city government in their infinite wisdom thought it best that we be "bused" across town. So, we walked six blocks to the city bus stop, was driven 10-12 miles to the subway station, took the subway way across Brooklyn to the Pennsylvania Avenue station, East-New York section of Brooklyn, then walked more blocks to a what we termed as a "slum school" with several thousand students on two separate sessions, one attending early in the morning, and one later in the day. Of course, we had the early morning session. This was done all to accommodate a building that was designed for only half the number of students attending, and to placate a collection of idiot politicians. It was a tough school, the scene of several murders by students on other students. Nice. More often than not, when the subway doors opened at the Pennsylvania Avenue station we stayed on the train, went to Manhattan and went to music stores, or the movies. Never did tell my parents.

My family was of Italian-Sicilian extraction, both sides. The grandparents came to America when they were young, about the late 1890's. Half went to New York/New Jersey, the other half went to Boston. I had great parents, loving, caring, and stable. The family, uncles, aunts, cousins, would always get together on holidays or summer visits. It was as much a celebration of the family as of the holiday. Some where Republicans, some where Democrats but, there was never an argument. There was a national consensus back then. Unlike today, we all agreed on the basics. You know, freedom of opportunity, free speech, the chance to get ahead; what they lacked in the old country. They all had WW 2, and the depression, fresh in their minds. Some were a bit liberal, some a little more conservative. But they all loved America. They were all hard working, rational, traditional Americans. They all believed in the American way, the system. To talk down America was unthinkable.

My kin were all working class. My father, uncle, brother-in-law, cousin, were either barbers or hairdressers. None went to college or even dreamed of that possibility. It was not that they were not smart. They were in their own way. However, this was an Italian American family that spoke two languages at dinner time. Doctors, lawyers, professors, professionals were looked upon with a certain degree of suspicion and awe. There were not many professionals in the family. My mother's cousin did marry a real estate lawyer. Her other cousin married a doctor. Good people, but we didn't see them much. Professionals were looked upon as upper-

3

class snobs who forgot the family and distanced themselves from the working class. The fear my family felt deeply.

My first experience with the law was the summer of '62 when we were playing with firecrackers and cherry bombs. A friend threw a cherry bomb in a sewer just when a cop car pulled up and asked us what we were doing. "Nothin." Then, the bomb went off and sprayed water all over the cop car. We were escorted into the cop car driven around and lectured by the cop. He let us go. Never did tell the parents about that either. The second experience was the rare occasion that my mother's cousin came to the house with her lawyer husband. I inquired as to the legal profession and was not encouraged. I thought being a trial lawyer would be fun. I was told criminal lawyers make no money since criminals rarely have any. After all, he was a real estate lawyer, was quite successful, even though one of the five families blew up his office for a professional and personal slight. Being a lawyer was a distant and far away dream. "It won't happen."

Close to home there was this fancy nightclub that our parents told us not to go near. It was called the Bamboo Lounge. My father told us that gangsters and prostitutes hung out there and that it was an unsavory place. So, of course, me, my brother and my friends went there as often as we could on Friday and Saturday nights peeking through the windows. We got to see and hear some of the musicians playing rock and jazz. It was lots of fun. It all ended when the club had a fire, and it was no more. I told my dad about the accidental fire. "Yes, it was an accident," he said.

I had a musical family. Mom played the piano by ear, my uncle played the saxophone, my cousin was also quite talented. This was the sixties, the age of the Beatles, Rolling Stones, etc. My friends and I formed a band. Did we practice! Every night, every weekend, we played in our den, with the blessings of mom and dad. "At least they are not hanging out or getting into trouble". We got pretty good. By the time of

4

High School, we were playing six nights a week at a posh Manhattan club called "Harlow's," making real money. We even signed a contract with United Artists and JATA Enterprises (management organization formed by a famous sixties group, "Jay and The Americans"). We were booked to play as backup band to some very unforgettable artists. We played backup to Patty Labelle and the Blue Bells (she was a lady), Chuck Berry (nasty), JJ Jackson (fun), and many, many others. It was an incredible experience. How many kids would have the opportunity to sit backstage with Rod Stewart (a gentleman), the Buckinghams, Billy Davis, Jr., Marilyn McCoo of the Fifth Dimension (very kind), Wilson Pickett (funny), Chuck Berry, etc., and just chat?! It was the era of sex, drugs and rock and roll. Some good times.

Drugs were used as a pastime experience by many and a terrible habit by others, especially rock stars. It affected their performances, their relationships with many, and often got them into trouble. The stories I could tell. Drugs was something I largely stayed away from. I knew it to be trouble and knew it would affect my health. It doesn't take being a rocket scientist to realize that taking drugs on a regular basis would eventually kill you. It was also an expensive habit. Because of the cost, I never even started to smoke cigarettes.

One incident affected me deeply and has influenced my practice of law. As ideal a childhood as I had, it was not perfect. I had an older first cousin who I was quite close to. He was a terrific musician and well thought of. Once, in the late sixties, I caught him in my bedroom shooting up heroin. I was stunned. He told me not to tell anyone, and that he needed it to get by. I told him he was only killing himself with that stuff. I told no one and have regretted it all my life. In the late nineties, my cousin called me on the phone from his home in Connecticut. He was suffering from hepatitis C, and severe liver damage. In short, he was dying. He cried like a baby on that phone. It broke my heart. I loved that man. But he said,

"I have no one to blame but myself." He died three weeks later. Drugs are bad, awfully bad. All this legalizing of drugs you see in many states will cause nothing but more dying cousins. Not a good idea.

This was also the Vietnam War protest, weather underground, SDS era. After speaking to many of these rock stars, it seemed to me that many were ill informed. Perhaps ill-informed is not an accurate description. Many were just plain stupid and hadn't a clue. They were just going along for the ride. I learned a lot about that side of life. Some of it was good, some of it was bad, very bad.

My third experience with the law was in Connecticut back in 1968, coming home from a gig in Branford. It was late at night, we were all hungry, went to a restaurant wherein I was picked on by a group of young thugs who had too much to drink. They picked on the wrong guy. One was knocked cold by a punch to the jaw and the second was thrown through a glass wall and seriously injured. By the time I got to the third, a half dozen cops showed up and I was confronted with an M-1 carbine. I was charged with felony assault. In court, the charges were dropped since the restaurant employees testified that I was defending myself from three intoxicated shitheads who had started the fight, and that the other band mates had left me there alone to deal with the situation. I often wonder whether that arrest and criminal action is still on record. I hate bullies.

My fourth experience with the law was in 1970 when a business manager owed me several thousand dollars and refused to pay what was owed. Wow, this really angered my dad in a big way! He refused to let it go and told me he would take care of it. What that meant, I was not sure. I received a phone call days later from a stranger who inquired as to the problem. I was told to be at the debtor's Manhattan apartment at a certain time. I asked my dad what this was all about. My dad told me to just do what the man said. I guess my dad owed some favors for all the crates of bootleg cigarettes that were stored in his garage. I did so and went to that Central Park apartment. Several minutes later, two expensive big cars pulled up and four well- dressed men exited the vehicles. After speaking with me for a few seconds they asked me to point out the apartment. One rang the buzzer of the glass door. When the debtor came down the stairs to inquire as to his visitors, he was told to open the door to discuss the problem. He refused. Another gentleman pulled out a pistol, placed it muzzle first on the door and again was told to open the "f----- door." He did. I was told to stay outside. They all went upstairs. They came down 15 minutes later. I was paid in full.

At this point in my life, I thought it best to have a backup career. My dad kept telling me the party is going to be over some day, and I'm going to have to earn a real living. My last experience told me he may be right. I did not know what to do. But it occurred to me that since I loved to watch my Sicilian grandma cook that I should try the culinary industry. I attended New York City Community College for nearly two years for Hotel and Restaurant management. The first year was all culinary art. I sure loved that. To this day I do most of all the cooking in my household. Wow, I can make a genuine New York Cheesecake, with no cracks! Move over Goodfella Henry Hill, my pasta sauce from scratch is the real thing. You got to use onions in that sauce! And the carbonara? Forget about it!

But still, a music career was still my first choice. Back in 1971, I thought it best to leave New York and find better opportunities in San Francisco, California. It was a beautiful, well-groomed city back then. My experiences there were mixed. I continued with my music career, played with some incredible jazz musicians on Union Street, but became increasingly disenchanted. At one point in time, I had no money, no job, no income and was sleeping in the back seat of my VW bug in a remote area in San Francisco. I understand the situation one finds himself in when homeless. What I do not understand is the mind set of those who revel in it, or politicians who accept it, as a permanent lifestyle for the "victims" of a free society. San Francisco is not what it used to be.

This was not a productive and happy experience. I lived in that car for over two weeks waiting for my "white privilege to kick in," to paraphrase Adam Carolla. But I found a job at a McDonald's and over time earned enough to support myself and pay the rent on a small apartment in the Western Addition. It was not a luxury apartment to say the least. In fact, I could still hear the pests scratching in the walls. In all my hardships, as a young man, far away from home, I never asked my parents for a penny. I never even asked the government to support me. Unlike many young people today, I was far too proud, far too independent to ask for help. I was going to live or die on my own terms, at my own speed. Some of my "terms" were not all together above board but hunger and survival can be an incredible motivator.

Crime and the bad stuff were never far away. When you live on the margins, you can expect some shit. I became a victim when a man with a .45 pistol showed up at the Fish and Chips shop I worked at and demanded the money in the till. I knew most of the cash was under the register and all that was in the till was a $100. I gave him only $100. The funny thing about that incident was that it did not scare me at all. The girls I worked with were crying as we all were led inside the refrigerator and were told to wait 15 minutes before opening the door. I was cracking snide remarks to the man, and he threatened to shoot me. In my Brooklyn neighborhood and Sicilian culture, stick up men were held in low esteem. They were losers. I again became a victim, about a year later in San Francisco, when I was held up with a gun yet again and demanded cash. I had none and they let me go. It happened a third time in San Francisco, when a 14-year-old kid presented me with a zip gun while I was working at a lunch counter. He thought better of it when he saw his city bus leaving without him. This was a low point in my life. I did a lot of thinking about my life and my future, or lack of future to be specific.

In 1973, at age 25, I decided to seek an education. But I did not even have a high school diploma. A community college tested me and was told I should do well in college. And did well, I did. I worked nearly full time as a shoe salesman, a cabinet maker, and lunch counter attendant while attending school. After all, some of us had no money, and no family to pay their way. My life experiences told me that if you have a "dream, motivation and an alarm clock", you can achieve anything. (I got that phrase from a rocker friend). After all, this is America! Success for some is not without pitfalls. Some must work to earn the money to pay for books, tuition, fees, living expenses, etc. Some of us had problems, including learning disabilities such as dyslexia, to overcome. But as my dad said, if you want something bad enough you can get it if you are willing to pay the price tag. For some, like me, we must pay quite a bit more than others.

There are those who believe that mere "chance" plays an important part in life, that success is not entirely because of one's own efforts. I believe that view of life is very much overstated and can be an obstacle to success. Oh, sure, I have had many "chance" obstacles on my way to secure the opportunities of the life I chose. But I have never permitted such happenings to block my goal. Many people experience similar obstacles and "chance" happenings. The ones that make it are the ones that figure out a way around it, or through it. I have always found a way to overcome them, some quite difficult and troublesome. In my experience, if you believe in yourself, and in a higher power that can and will give you comfort in hard times, you can create your own opportunities.

If you believe that you may not make it by some "chance" happening, you just may not try hard enough. That spells death to success.

Starting college at age 25 was difficult. More so if you have no study skills, poor grammar, and poor writing skills. By my senior year at San Francisco State, I was a tutor to the foreign students who had difficulty with writing English, civics, and American history. Most of these students were refugees from the Vietnam war and came from Cambodia, Laos, Thailand. I grew to have a tremendous respect for these people since they had developed a remarkable willingness and ability to work hard to achieve success considering the disabilities and disadvantages, they had to endure. I was also chosen to be the student-teacher liaison in the History Department.

It never failed to amaze me that if you are motivated to learn and succeed, teachers pick up on that and are more than happy to bend over backwards for you. Some of these teachers and professors I knew had no patience with those who wanted to take the easy way out or were just marking time. One professor I knew carried a "crying towel" with him for those who would not take responsibility for themselves, when they failed an exam. In those days, there were no "safe spaces" for those students to hide. Some, as many are today, were quite willing and happy to give students passing grades for little or no work simply because they believed that student was a "victim" of this or that. To my mind, they did no favors to those students. Life can be tough. If you are not prepared for it, you simply melt.

Life at a cable car college like San Francisco State was both eye-opening, if not confusing. My background was one of accepting responsibility for oneself, by knowing that life does not owe you a living or success. I found far too many students had different ideas and most came from well to do families, whose families were picking up the tab for all the expenses for their numbskull kids. Even back then I heard plenty of excuses. They gave no more than what they were willing to give, and it wasn't much.

In college, I also heard a great deal of anger. Anger at what? So many of these kids had it all. They had mom and dad paying all their expenses, their books, their autos, money for dating, and plenty of beer. I had none of those things given to me. I should have been angry, but I never was. In fact, I felt lucky to have been there on the road to a degree. I was far too busy trying to succeed and no time being angry. It never even occurred to me that I should be angry, except perhaps, at them for being angry. I never thought I was owed anything. But then again, I began to understand that their anger came from emulating their teachers and professors who were angry at everything capitalist. Their possibilities for success and achievement were everywhere.   I never understood those people. Still don't.

One teacher affected me in a profound way. She was a political science professor teaching political systems, philosophies, etc. The course was advertised as "classical philosophy." Ok, great, I can learn all about Socrates, Plato, whatever. But the course was not as advertised. On the first day of class, she perused through her wallet and showed us her membership card in the American Communist Party. What was taught was simply Marxism, Soviet style and Maoism, and the joys of being a communist. I was stunned by what she taught and even more stunned by the empty minded students who never challenged anything she said. Never seen so many slack-jawed young people in my life. Talk about indoctrination! I was the only one who challenged everything she said, to the point that she refused to acknowledge my raised hand, or even my presence. She did insist that sooner or later America would go to the extreme left, and that they would do "whatever it takes" to get there. Hmmm. I absorbed all the information taught, took it all in and learned about them, their methods, and goals. She did have integrity. I was the only student who received an A from her course.

At San Francisco State, it occurred to me that "my God, I could become a lawyer!" That possibility seemed achievable. Sure, I had no money and no help, but this could be done, if I worked hard enough. I mean, I had straight A's at San Francisco State and great letters from professors. But I had to take the LSAT (law school admissions test) to gain admission to a good school and we all knew I was lousy at these exams. I took the exam, did lousy. Somehow, I had to overcome that learning disability dyslexia wherein I would reverse the questions on the exam and answer "yes" rather than "no." I managed to attend some sessions with a therapist who specialized in that sort of stuff. I did better the second time around but still not great. Still, two schools wanted to see me personally for an interview to explain how I could do so well at San Francisco State and do so badly on the admissions test. I was thrilled they wanted to see me! One law professor told me that "they would find a seat for me at the law school." Next to passing the Bar, one of the happiest moments of my life. As a footnote the American Bar Association has withdrawn any support for the LSAT, stating that it is not a good indicator of success in law school. Go figure.

In my senior year, I was accepted to two law schools, one in DC and one in Southern California. San Diego sounded more attractive. It was an exceedingly difficult three years since I had to work to earn a living to attend law school. In my third year of law school, I clerked for a criminal lawyer in San Diego who had a unique criminal trial practice, representing an exclusive clientele in Southern California and Las Vegas. I have an enormous respect for this man and his skills. He was so smooth. He taught me a great deal. I owe him a lot. Later, I was also certified by my law school with the State Bar to appear in court under the supervision of a practicing lawyer with the United States Attorney's office. I didn't like it.

I received my J.D. degree in 1980. My Sicilian parents went to the ceremony in San Diego. They were both enormously proud, if not stunned. I moved back to the Bay Area to complete the Bar requirements and practice law. I chose litigation. Coming from Brooklyn, I have always liked combat, but mostly I felt it was the best way to help the people I wanted to help and to achieve a certain independence. I was much older than other new lawyers and a bit more mature. Besides, I like being my own boss. Perhaps I don't play well with others!

Practicing law as a sole practitioner takes a great deal of spunk. Face it, in most cases you're up against the big boys, the law firms, both private and governmental, with numerous lawyers, unlimited budgets, and unlimited ways they can trip you up. But that is what I chose to do. I like independence and mostly I like choosing the cases that interest me. You must have a strong stomach and not fear your opposition. I know that is easy to say, but your confidence will come as you increase your experience. I opened a law office in the Bay Area. I actually secured a loan from a bank from just my membership card in the California State Bar. The wages of ambition, opportunity and hard work is success!

2

How It All Works or The View from The Trench

Understanding the legal system can be of great benefit to those who find themselves having to deal with it. Sooner or later, everyone confronts the legal system. The more you know about it, the less painful it may be. It's like a doctor who tells you this or that poking around will hurt. It may still hurt, but at least you know it's coming. The courts are not chaotic or without protocols. Correct legal procedures or court rules are everything, whether it be criminal, civil, or family law. "Notice and an opportunity to be heard" is the very essence of all Anglo-American jurisprudence. Procedure, what can be expected, takes time. There will be no rush to judgment in the Court system. At the same time, the wheels of justice will invariably turn slowly. The procedures described here are basic and may be somewhat different from state to state. But you get the big picture. In this brief synopsis, I will not describe the appeals process. That is a different ball game altogether, and beyond the scope of this book. Happily, I have had to take only four cases to the Court of Appeals. Three were won, one was lost. Not too bad.

Criminal law is rather basic and revolves around fairness to the defendant, coupled with protecting the public. Once an individual is arrested and charged with a crime, the procedure will depend on whether the crime charged is a felony or a misdemeanor. Misdemeanor charges, such as driving under the influence, petty theft, simple assault, and many, many others, will involve an arraignment in a lower court. Mostly, a Circuit Court. The person charged will hear the charge and be asked to plead. The Defendant will be asked to seek an attorney, or one will be appointed for him. At the arraignment, the pre-trial conference date will be given, as well as the trial date. The pre-trial will usually be two weeks before the trial. The judge will set bail, either cash, surety, or signature.

At this stage, the defense attorney will serve on the District Attorney a Discovery Request for all evidence in the case. This would include police reports, witness statements, video tapes, audio tapes, laboratory reports, and so on. It is at this stage that the lawyer will analyze the case. Depending upon the lawyer the defendant chooses, of course, the lawyer may simply ask the client as to his culpability. But all lawyers will analyze the stop and detention, the search warrant, and warrantless search, the arrest, as to whether it meets constitutional requirements. If it does not, the lawyer will file a motion to exclude all evidence of the improper search or arrest. This may include any and all evidence seized, the confession, and/or statements made, and so on. Usually, the motion to exclude the evidence will also include a motion to dismiss the case, since if there is no proper evidence, there can be no case. I have done this in a number of cases. Sometimes, the police simply make mistakes.

It is then the lawyer and the client must make a decision regarding disposition. It should be noted that even if a guilty plea is the only alternative, every defendant has some mitigating circumstance as to culpability that might help in the disposition. It should be noted that some cases have aggravating circumstances that simply do not help. The defendant may plead guilty to the crime charged or plead to a lesser offense. A fine may be imposed or a jail sentence if the crime is serious enough. The court will always surcharge court costs and victim compensation. The Court will even give the defendant time to pay the fine and charges.

In some cases, where the defendant has no prior convictions, and is a good candidate, the Court will permit a deferment. That is, the client pleads guilty to the charge, and after a short probation, usually six months, the court will dismiss the charges! Scott free! No record at all. This is a once in a lifetime opportunity. I have actually had clients who declined and wanted to use it for more serious offenses! I was always suspicious of that decision.

Felony cases are more serious and involve resolutions that could affect your future employment. Your initial appearance will also be in a Circuit Court. There you will be advised of your rights, bail will be set, and a date for a preliminary hearing will be set. The preliminary Hearing is also called a Probable Cause hearing, in that the court must determine whether the defendant probably committed the crime. This hearing can be waived. However, I usually opt for the hearing, since it is the best way to determine what evidence the prosecuting attorney has on my client, and whether his witnesses are credible.

At the hearing, the officers will testify and any other pertinent witnesses. This is one of the few times hearsay types of evidence can be used to determine probability. Defense attorneys will have the opportunity to cross-examine these witnesses and to even present their own evidence. Defense lawyers will do so to try and knock out a count or two. Some lawyers don't present much evidence lest they give away their defense case. Each case is different. Use your best judgement. The Defendant is usually bound over for trial and the case transferred to the District Court. That's the Court for the big boys.

The Defendant will be arraigned in the District Court and the matter will eventually be set for trial. The Constitution has "speedy trial" provisions, so it must be set within a certain period of time, unless defendant's counsel waives time for trial, then the case may be extended. At the initial appearance in District Court, bail may be reset or modified. After this appearance, the Discovery requests are the same, as are the materials asked for and received. It is at this point that counsel may consult with experts on any relevant issue at trial. The same meet and confer with the client will take place to determine a fair disposition. At this point. The client may ask for a change of plea or a setting for trial.

If the client chooses to change his plea considering all the alternatives, I will ask for a pre-plea probation report, especially if your client has little in the way of a criminal background. Getting the probation department on your side is a big plus. In felony cases I have found that a lengthy sentencing hearing is more than appropriate, rather, it is a necessity. I have retained experts for these hearings, have called witnesses, and have admitted all sorts of documents to show the court that there are mitigating circumstances that the Court needs to consider before sentencing the defendant. I have found that that this works very well, and I have almost always had my sentence requests honored. Experts are great. Judges love it when someone else is responsible for making the decisions.

Civil cases also have strict protocols and procedures and the same "fair notice and opportunity to be heard," governs. A civil complaint is filed with the Court that would include causes of action, be it breaches of contract, negligence, personal injury, trespass, quite title to real property, breach of fiduciary duties, wrongful death, almost any imaginable harm that someone has allegedly done to another.

17

Once filed, the complaint is personally served with a Summons, informing the defendant, that he must file and Answer or Response within 30 days (In Wyoming it is 20 Days). This gives time for the Defendant to seek counsel. Almost invariably, there is not enough time to respond to the Complaint and additional give is requested and almost always it is given. There is such a thing as professional courtesy.

The response to the Complaint can be a straight up Answer, or a Motion to Dismiss for any number of reasons or, in California, a Demurrer (a "so what" response). After the pleading stage is finished, and the issues defined, the Discovery process begins. This may take as little as a few months to as long as several years, depending on the case and its complexity. Of course, each party wants the world from the other party, and will ask for any and all "relevant" documents, tapes, videos, bank accounts, investment accounts, mortgages, deeds, you name it. This is when it gets sticky, and some parties try to harass their opponents with over broad discovery. Most courts I know will schedule a Status Conference to bring all parties together to work out any discovery problems, or whatever other problems they are confronted with. Depositions will be scheduled, written interrogatories and Requests to Admit will be served.

After the discovery phase is completed, the parties are looking at the clock since by that time the trial date has already been set. The Court may order a mediation in the matter in front of the trial, to dispose of the case without expending expensive court time. If no disposition can be had, then a trial is in the offing. Be prepared, no one can ever predict what a jury will do, no matter how good you think your case is.

Family law is not unlike civil law. The same procedures apply in that a Complaint for Dissolution will be filed, and will ask to distribute property, child custody and visitation issues to be determined, spousal support and/or retirement funds distributed. California is a community property no fault state,

18

and the court will distribute the property accumulated during the marriage equally to each no matter who was at fault. Wyoming is an "equitable distribution" state, and will distribute the property, all the property, "equitably." What "equitably" means is subject to a judge's discretion. That discretion is broad, and the property distribution could very well be unequal. Civil discovery rules will also apply here.

The real problems come with child custody and visitation issues. In California, mediation became required. The parents were compelled to sit down with a qualified mediator and decide the future of their children. In Wyoming mediation is not mandatory but only encouraged. Not good enough, as far as I am concerned. Once custody and visitation are agreed upon, it is put into a Child custody and visitation agreement and made an order of the court. But understand that custody and visitation is an issue that never dies, except on the child reaching age eighteen, or until they graduate from high school. It can always be revisited by the court on a motion for a change in circumstances. This is when things become complicated, emotional, and the fighting continues.

No description of the family law legal system can be complete without a word about spousal support, or what some states call "alimony." California loves spousal support and will award it liberally. All you need is to ask and state your need, describe the diverse differences in income, the quality of life you are used to, and the length of your marriage and you're in. In Wyoming, well, forget it. Wyoming does have a spousal support statute, but support is rarely awarded. Wyoming is a state that believes that both parties need to earn their own living, and in the notion that if you are going to split and divorce, and separate forever, then all the ties should be cut. There is a certain logic to that perspective.

The following cases discussed here state facts that are all within the public court files and/or stated in open court on the record. Some cases are included to educate the public as to how the courts deal and dispose of various cases and issues in both California and in Wyoming. Some cases are included which are downright funny and amusing. Grunt lawyers know full well that no matter how well they prepare for a court hearing some issues and matters are simply not foreseeable. Lawyers are sometimes the victim of the unexpected, especially when they throw the dice. Some cases start out in a serious vein but end in a laugh riot. One of the side effects of being a Grunt Lawyer.

3
Cutting Your Teeth

One of the problems for a young lawyer is gaining the court room experience needed by a litigator. Sure, you can read up on it, you can watch other lawyers in a big law firm, but at one time or another, you must get out there and do it yourself. Some lawyers try to take law school courses in trial practice, and that is good. But the real thing is different. It just is. There is a certain aura about real courtrooms and real cases with real people, real problems, and real opponents that trial practice cannot duplicate. You cannot duplicate emotions.

You can prepare just so many wills to keep your head above water. When I started my practice, a neighbor lawyer was an experienced attorney who specialized in Contractor's License laws. He represented a large contractor's license bonding surety company and was their lead lawyer. They issued surety bonds to contractors that were required by California law. These bonds secured against a contractor's conduct on the job that could be considered "willful and deliberate violations of the contractor's license law." We are not talking about negligence here. We are talking about "willful and deliberate" conduct that can loosen up the bonding company to pay the bond amount to the recipient of the contractor's conduct.

I was asked by this lawyer if I could travel around the state and make all his court appearances for him regarding these bonds. The appearances were, in effect, trials on the bond, as to whether the contractors' conduct could be considered "willful and deliberate" violations of the law. The way the law was written it was difficult for the plaintiffs to collect on the bond because the statutory standard of willfulness was so high. I had to travel all over the state to small rural counties, to large cities and suburbs, and represent that surety bonding company in many trials. I jumped at the chance I was offered. This was a terrific opportunity to get the experience I needed. After dozens of trials all over the state, I became quite comfortable in court.

What was so sad was that many contractors simply did a lousy job on the homes they were contracted to construct, but the property owners could not collect on the bond because the court, as much as it wanted to, could not find the requisite willful violation of the contractor's license law. A showing of negligence was not enough. In many cases the contractor failed to pay the subcontractors, even when he was paid by the property owner, because he pocketed the money, or that he under-bid the job, and walked off the job. In those cases, I simply found that to be willful, and instructed the company to pay on the bond.

In one case, the contractor was hired to rebuild the foundation of an old four-story brownstone in the East Bay. The contractor had to lift the building in such a way as to put in a new foundation. He did so. But when he did, it was done so incorrectly that the entire building slid off the lifts and tumbled into the neighboring building! This was truly a disaster. Not only was the building destroyed but the building next to it as well. So, they sued the contractor on the bond.

The damage was in the hundreds of thousands of dollars. But the bond that was required by the State of California to secure a contractor's license was only $5,000! It did not end well.

Today, the surety bond is only $15,000. As we all know, $15,000 doesn't buy much in construction costs. It is usually a drop in the old bucket. These surety bonds are basically for small jobs, not large new construction projects. To my mind there were far too many people who should have been compensated by the bonding company but were not because of the strict interpretation of the phrase "willful and deliberate." As the lead lawyer of the surety company would say to me when I left for a trial: "Good luck, Rob. Maybe justice will prevail, and we'll lose."

4

The Scared Old Widower

This case came to me from another lawyer who refused it. "Not enough money in the case," he said. The defendant was an older gentleman, about age 65, who was stopped and detained by a California Highway Patrol officer on the Oakland-San Francisco Bay Bridge for suspicion of driving drunk. The gentleman had never been arrested in his life, had a clean driving record. It was about 12:00 midnight, was rather cold with light traffic. A typical summer night in San Francisco. The CHP officer stated in his report that the defendant was weaving and not in his lane. The stop was apparently good. They didn't have video recorders back then. But since the officer's report stated that the driver's vehicle was weaving in and out of lane and the defendant had no other witnesses there goes the motion to suppress the evidence and a possible dismissal. The defendant was given a field sobriety test (FST), walk the line, finger to nose, etc., and it was determined that the defendant was intoxicated. The old guy was arrested, handcuffed, and brought to the San Francisco County Jail (a bad place. It smells of urine in there). At the jail, defendant was given a machine breathalyzer test in which it was found he had a .16 BAL (blood alcohol level). Pretty high BAL, since at that time a .10 was considered intoxicated. Today a .08 will get you arrested.

Wow. Sounds like an open and shut case. But I took the case anyway. I was relatively new at the Bar; I needed the experience. Besides the man did not have much money and I was quite sympathetic. I was all he could afford. He was the original "sad sack." He had recently lost his wife of 36 years to cancer, had little income, always seemed depressed. Maybe I could get a lower fine since he had no priors. But all cases, no matter how bad they sound, need to be investigated. You never know what you can find. My client told me he went to a dinner party in Berkeley with friends and acquaintances and had only two glasses of wine. I phoned all the participants at that dinner party and asked what was served at the dinner, both food and drink. All five said it was only white wine with chicken, rice, green beans, and a cheesecake for dessert. All five insisted my client only had two glasses of wine. Two of the participants never met my client until that evening and I believe had no incentive to lie to me.

Having two glasses of wine does not give you a .16 BAL, especially after eating a full meal, since food always absorbs alcohol. (Never drink on an empty stomach!) My experiences with alcohol told me the BAL should have been a .04 - ,05, maybe. Something was terribly wrong here. I consulted with a toxicologist about the fact pattern, sent him my file. He stated that he knew that particular BAL machine in San Francisco and knew it to be inaccurate since it was on a wobbly table and was susceptible to false readings because of greasy hands by the operator or whatever. I retained this expert to testify. I also subpoenaed the witnesses at that dinner party.

However, I still had that Officers' testimony in which the Officer determined defendant to be intoxicated because of the tests given and his weaving out of lane. On the day of trial, the CHP officer testified flawlessly. I mean, he was a professional witness. Probably testified dozens of times. He wore his impeccable CHP uniform, was a bit arrogant, and looked at the jury when he spoke. This guy was good. On day two it was my turn to cross-exam the officer. How in the world am I going to do this? How am I going to shake him up? I've got a jury of 12 in front of me, and a law school class comes into the courtroom to observe an actual criminal trial! Unless you have seen the Municipal Court rooms at San Francisco City Hall you don't know what fear is. The court rooms are magnificent and dignified, with high ceilings, multiple crown moldings, mahogany paneled walls, the whole thing. Like in the movies. I'm just a new lawyer feeling his way. Sometimes you think, "what am I doing here? I'm just a rookie." The judge made me feel better. He was an Afro-American judge, reality based, not complicated as some judges are. He gave me a lot of leeway. I really liked him. He was fair.

The female prosecutor examined the officer, at length. When she said that fateful statement, "no further questions," I knew it was my turn. The judge said: "Mr. DiLorenzo, your witness." Oh my, I better think of something. I stood up and asked the basic questions. How long have you been a CHP officer? What training? I went through the whole litany of the officer's qualifications. I wanted to show that this man was firm in his convictions via his training. I wanted to nail him down as to what had happened and how he saw it all. We went through the facts of the stop and detention, the fact that it was late at night, that it was cold on the bridge, etc. I asked about the defendant, how he was driving, how he stepped out of the car. His age, especially his age was important, as well as how he looked, his attitude, whether he was cooperative, whether he was nervous, whether the officer checked his criminal record, or not, etc.

But I wanted to concentrate on the field sobriety tests. I asked the officer which FST he asked my client to perform? The officer stated: "I asked him to perform the finger to nose test." " Did he perform the test," I asked? "Yes, but he failed the test." One could now anticipate the series of questions that I was going to ask. Here are my questions. "How did he fail the test?" "What did he do wrong?" "Did that failure indicate to you that defendant was drunk?" "Do you always ask a suspect to do the finger to nose test?" "Why?" "Because, in your experience, which I admit is extensive, it is to your mind a dependable indicator of sobriety, correct?" "Absolutely", he said. I asked specifically, "if Mr. B failed that test, did his failure of that test indicate to you he was, indeed, intoxicated?" "And you would arrest that man?" I asked. He said "yes." I had to corner this officer as to the positive dependability of the FST.

At that point I asked the officer to stand up, face the jury, and demonstrate the finger to nose test exactly as to how he expected the defendant to perform that test. "Objection" from the prosecutor. "Mr. DiLorenzo is just wasting time, it is common knowledge what a finger to nose test is," etc. The judge stated that he thought the jury is entitled to know how the test works. "Overruled."

Here is how this went down. I asked the officer to stand up and face the jury. He did so. (Me) "What did you ask the defendant to do?" (Officer) I asked defendant to stand at attention. (Me) Officer stand at attention. He stood at attention. (me) I asked defendant to lean back. (Me) "Officer, lean back." The Officer leaned back. (Officer) I asked the defendant to extend his arms. (Me) Officer, please extend your arms. (officer) I asked the defendant to close his eyes. (Me) Officer, please close your eyes. (Officer) I asked the defendant to extend his index finger and touch the tip of his nose with his index finger. (Me) Officer, please extend your index finger and touch the tip of your nose, exactly as you expected defendant to pass the FST? The officer did so. However, the Officer touched his right cheek rather than the tip of his nose! You would think we were at the New York Comedy Club in the East Village. The jury laughed, as well as the student audience. The judge tried hard to keep a straight face. The officer looked embarrassed.

I then asked the officer to retake the stand. You can all imagine the questions that were just waiting to be asked at this point. (Me) Officer, you did not touch the tip of your nose, did you? (Officer) "No." (Me) In fact, you touched your right cheek, correct? (Officer) Yes, I did. (Me) To correctly pass that test you were supposed to touch the tip of your nose, correct? (Officer) "Yes." (Me) But you did not, correct? (Officer) Yes, I did not. (Me) Officer, you failed that FST, did you not? (Officer) Yes, I did. (Me) Officer, you came into this courtroom in an intoxicated condition, did you not!? (Officer) No, I haven't had a drink in weeks.

Oh, the laughter in that court room. We went through the litany of how "dependable" the FST is. The arrogant officer was taken completely by surprise, was disarmed and was naked before the court. His credibility was lost, and the jury saw and heard a whole new side of DUI field protocols.

Look, I do not imply to suggest any lawyer use this tactic. It is way too troublesome and uncertain. It violates a maxim that you never ask a question unless you know the answer to be given. But there are times when desperation takes over and you must throw the dice. The State had a BAL of .16, they had the Officer's testimony, and, they had testimony as to how dependable the test results are. I had a sad sack defendant, the people at the dinner party in which the jury could believe may have been biased, and all I had was a toxicologist who believed the machine was wrong and inaccurate. Sometimes you got to do what you got to do.

During closing, I made a big deal out of the failure of the Officer to pass his own FST, the fact that he argued it was flawless and dependable, etc. I argued that the Officer failed the field sobriety test not because he was intoxicated, (which surely, he was not) but because people who are nervous fail them all the time. The man was put in a situation of performing in front of a full court room, in front of a jury, in front of a robed judge. Sure, the Officer was as nervous as my client was when he was stopped. Anyone would be. Just imagine, I argued, you are 65 years old, pulled over in the middle of the night by a CHP officer, have never been stopped before, are elderly, and on a cold night on the San Francisco-Oakland Bay Bridge. The man was naturally extremely nervous and very scared. Sure, he failed the test. Anyone, under those set of circumstances would fail the FST. Your nerves are shot. You don't think straight, your frazzled, under stress. Sober people fail those FST's all the time. The FST's are not a good indicator of sobriety. At most it is a suggestion, a maybe.

After over five days at trial the jury retired to deliberate. The judge did state that this trial was the longest DUI jury trial in San Francisco history, and that they usually last only two days. The jury deliberated for quite some time. The District Attorney kept walking in and conferring with the deputy as to the results since the trial was taking so long, and the deputy was needed elsewhere. The female deputy was concerned. She was not happy with me. The jury came back several times with no verdict. The result was a hung jury. No conviction. As any trial lawyer knows, a mistrial is as good as a win. The state did not want to retry the case. Too much court time. Case dismissed!

I felt good about it all. So much so that I went to a local pub near the courthouse that lawyers frequent and had a beer. I did it. I survived it all. Not only that, I succeeded! To be clear, I have the highest regard for law enforcement officers, especially that CHP officer. Many of my close friends are in law enforcement. They have a tough job, are not given enough credit for what they must deal with, and in many quarters, especially these days, are not respected. This is not only unfortunate but is dangerous. Police officers are like lawyers, when you need one, you're glad they are around. In all my years of law practice, I have very rarely ever found an officer who actually and purposely lied and tried to falsify evidence. Sometimes they do make mistakes. Prosecutors are another story.

What did I learn from this matter? Sometimes the obvious is not so obvious. Sometimes you must dig a little. I was always under the impression that a breathalyzer test was a dependable indicator of BAL. Not so. It has many variables, not only within the machine itself, but the operator who uses it. It can and sometimes does give a false reading. If you are in that situation, ask for a blood test. Those tests are 98% accurate. Secondly, I learned that FST are not inherently reliable. You must go beyond the FST. What is reliable are the witnesses to the drinking, what he ate, the amount of alcohol consumed, and the length of time from the last drink to the chemical test. None of it made sense and that is why the case was taken to trial.

Did I get paid for my services, for all the investigation and research efforts, for the retainer of an expert, for trial preparation, staying up till midnight to formulate a closing argument, and seven days in trial? Yes, very much. That trial cost my client about $2,000. Talk about bargain basement. It was all he could afford. Was it worth it? You bet it was. I received a lifetime of experience in that trial and a satisfaction you cannot put a price tag on.

5

Girls Just Want to Have Fun

This case was short and sweet. It never went to trial. Never even went to a hearing, other than an initial appearance for a plea. It was fun nevertheless and proved to be quite an embarrassment to a big city Police Department. When the client came to see me, I was impressed by the fact that she was forthright and candid. She cried and we had the usual attorney-client conversation. She was a very pretty lady, about 21 years old, Hispanic, going to college away from home. The midterm exams were finished, and they wanted to celebrate. She was genuinely concerned about her parents finding out that she had been arrested with her cousin. It was obvious she came from a nice family and that they were proud their daughter was going to college. She kept asking me if her parents would be notified. I told her no, that she was over age for any notification of the parents. I assured her I would do all I could to keep the matter quiet.

She told me the facts and was crying while doing so. It seems she was terribly embarrassed by what had happened, and that it was terribly out of character for her. "I wasn't raised this way!" Well, in any case, the court records state that she and her cousin go to a nightclub to go dancing and drink a little bit. However, as the police report states, she and her

31

cousin didn't drink a little bit, in fact they drank a lot. They meet a man and start talking to him at the bar. The man is good looking and after a while propositions my client. She accepts, albeit reluctantly, stating that he seemed like a nice guy. My client, the man and my client's cousin, end up at a motel. The man wants both girls in bed! They say no. However, this man is sly and insistent and offers to pay them $100.00. All three of them strip, get into bed, wherein he starts fondling the girls. After several minutes of this, the door is busted open, and the girls are charged with prostitution.

I got the case from the Public Defender's Office. It seems they cannot take my client's case because they were representing my client's cousin in the same case. They had a classic conflict of interest. I read the police reports, consulted with both girls, with the permission of the PD's office, as to the facts of that night. I determined that what happened here is a classic entrapment. It was the police officer who originated the idea of the crime and induced my client to engage in it. Besides, my client never agreed to the $100. It certainly was not my client's idea. But somehow the police reports do not tell all the facts. It failed to mention that the $100 offer of payment was the officer's idea, that all three were in bed naked for some time before the bust. This leaves the officers' going above and beyond the call of duty.

A pretrial conference was held, and we had an interesting conversation with the Deputy DA and the judge. I made my pitch to the judge telling him the facts as I saw them and as I would prove in court. The DA, being honest, did admit the officers were far too enthusiastic with their job, and that he did not think he could prove that the idea of the crime did not originate with the officer. After the laughter at the visualizations of the cop in bed with the two girls, and the jokes told by us all, the judge was a bit put out and insistent that no crime had taken place and that the officers in the matter played fast and loose with the facts. The judge was also quite annoyed with the fact that the officer was far too enthusiastic with his role in the scenario, by stripping naked, and crawling into bed with these two young ladies.

This was one of the few cases I handled in which the officers could have been more candid. They were not. In fact, I was annoyed the case went this far. The officers were veteran officers, not their first rodeo, and knew better. The case was eventually dismissed for both ladies. I must admit that there was a great deal of laughter in those chambers as to the conduct of the defendants and the officers. In our business you capitalize on all the humor you can find.

The client was incredibly pleased with the result. She was especially glad that her mom would never find out about her indiscretion. Both ladies, I believe, learned a lesson they will never forget. The lesson learned by me was that you must go beyond the police reports. Sometimes the police make mistakes. Sometimes they are not as candid as they could be. I believed my client. After a while you will become a good judge of people, their credibility, and the facts that surround the matter.

6
Take That to The Bank

This was a big-league case, and the first time I had to deal with the FBI. Dealing with the FBI is never a happy experience. The defendant was the Vice President of a big national bank in San Francisco. The man was sophisticated and wealthy. He lived in a very opulent part of the county in a house that could be described as a mansion. I met with him and his beautiful wife at his home. They were both well spoken, and genuinely concerned about the developments that were to overtake them. They had been visited by the FBI, which is never a pleasant experience. I insisted that if the FBI ever seeks another interview that they are not to do so without my being present. In the meantime, they were to not talk to anyone about the matter.

He was charged with misappropriation of bank funds. I was retained to represent the man. After hearing all the facts, and a review of the court file, I was a bit puzzled. The defendant did not steal any money as I saw it. The facts are that he and his wife had a job recruitment business on the side. A "headhunter" business. You recruit qualified people with the right qualifications for the right job in certain businesses. What they were doing was that they were recruiting qualified people to be employed at the national bank defendant was employed at. Of course, the employer bank would pay the recruitment fee, which was substantial, to the "headhunter" business for finding and delivering the qualified employee to the bank. At our interview, the client told me that the bank was hiring unqualified people who could not do the job. He thought he was doing the bank a favor by giving them qualified people that could be productive and valuable to his bank.

I figured at worse the defendant had a conflict of interest by not disclosing to the bank that he and his wife owned the business that was recruiting employees to the bank and receiving the big checks from the bank for services rendered. Besides, the employees recruited were highly qualified and the bank hired them. So, what's the problem? Boy, was I wrong. The FBI came down on my client like a sledgehammer. They kept arguing that they must "preserve the integrity of the national banking system."

FBI agents are a different breed. They are not what you think they are, or what the movies portray them as. For the most part they are not gun wielding agents like you see on TV, fighting crime in the streets, infiltrating the mob, or whatever. Some of that may be true, but for the most part, they are four-eyed nerds and dorks, with degrees as public accountants. Some of them just don't even look the part.

Defending a case against the federal government is no laughing matter. These guys will do near anything, whatever it takes, spend any money needed, to get a conviction. No wonder they have a conviction rate as high as 95% plus. That is worrisome in itself. As a defense lawyer you are in a precarious position, with limited funds to work with, limited hands to work on the matter, and in fact, you're up against the best. Your options are limited. You must either work to get an acquittal, a dismissal, or accept a lessor charged offense. You must do your homework, understand the crime charged, review past cases and precedent, review the evidence with witnesses, consult with the client, even consult with other attorneys. The FBI does not mess around. Ask Michael Flynn.

This case concerned me. Whenever you deal with the Feds be careful, very careful. I thought that since this was my first big Federal case. I should consult with a former Assistant U.S. Attorney who was in private practice as to the crime charged, my approach as to defenses, and the possible outcome. Lucky for me, such a man was practicing law next to my office, specializing in defective "boob cases." We had several discussions over the case, and he thought my approach was sound. After getting his seal of approval, I had to calculate the chances of getting an acquittal or a mistrial. How many times does that happen? I have always thought that my job as a lawyer must be to limit the amount of damage that can be inflicted on my client. That has always been upper most in my mind. Sometimes, to do that, you just have to be creative.

I had a long consultation with my client and asked if there was anything untowardly about this particular national bank. "What do you mean?" Did the bank to your mind do anything you believed to be improper? I have been told by the FBI far too many times about their desire to preserve the integrity of the national banking system so much so that I wanted to perhaps give the FBI another opportunity to preserve that integrity. My client said "well, the bank has repeatedly overcharged the Feds for services." Say what? The bank has overcharged the Federal government for certain services and products. I asked for particulars about these services and charges and heard a mouthful. Oh my. Time to talk to the FBI. I set up a meeting with the FBI at the United States Attorney's Office to discuss this. The FBI and the Feds wanted to know everything. And my client was willing to chat.

Now it becomes time to play that favorite lawyer parlor game "let's make a deal." And a deal we made.

My client served no time, no fine, the money paid was given back and the damages to himself, his family, and his life were circumscribed. It was a particularly good result. Even my former Assistant U.S. Attorney friend was surprised by the result. To this day, a lesson was learned, and such activities were never ever engaged in again. Sometimes you do what you have to do to get a good result. There are times when creativity can do the job. I have also found that the courts are sometimes more lenient with white collar offenses. I also learned that just because your client doesn't think that what he did was criminal doesn't mean he did not break the law. However, as compared to my upbringing, this was not a case in which my client was selling bootleg cigarettes out of the trunk of his car, or that he had "connections," or stuck a pistol in a door window.

Several years ago, this former client called me and told me a friend of his was charged with the same offense, except his lawyer took it all the way to trial and charged him a small fortune for that trial. He was found guilty and sentenced to prison for two years. He called to say thank you for the job I did and having the wisdom to figure out a way to plead it out with no jail time. One of the good feelings you get for a job well done, and a case with a good outcome for the client.

7

The New Age Mother

This was one of the most difficult matters I had to deal with. Just a lot of conflicting emotions in this one case. I received a call from a couple in Chicago who heard of me by way of a recommendation. These were fine people. They had a 19-year-old son who was in jail and charged with child molestation of a 9-year-old girl while he was renting a room in the child's home. Due to the nature of the crime, I don't normally take such cases, as well as rape crimes as I find them emotionally exhausting, and they tend to stay stuck in my head. The neat thing about private practice is that you do not need to take every case that comes through the door. You can pick and choose the matters you are interested in or in which you sincerely believe in the client or in his innocence. The phone call from the mother and father was so desperate, so heartfelt, that I at least should see and interview the client in the county jail and decide as to whether I would take the case or not.

I interviewed the 19-year- old the following day in the county jail. What I found was a "kid", well groomed, well spoken, and a polite, if immature young man in dire trouble. The interview was unremarkable. I was a bit suspicious.

The court file facts are these. The defendant was attending college and rented a room from the victim's mother, a successful medical doctor and professor at a leading university. The doctor, a female, in her 40's, apparently divorced and living with her 9-year-old daughter in a nice house, in a very affluent section of the county. The defendant told the authorities that he was constantly being disturbed and bothered by this precocious nine-year-old, that she would try to gain entrance to his room and in fact, he had to purchase a lock on the door to keep her out.

I found this to be a somewhat strange arrangement with this boarder and the doctor since the doctor had a hot tub which was used frequently by the doctor and her daughter. The doctor would always be completely naked with her daughter in the hot tub and would invite the defendant to join them, which he did on occasion. In fact, the doctor and her daughter appeared semi-naked on numerous occasions walking about the house. I thought this conduct to be rather bizarre, brainless, reckless behavior by the doctor and an invitation for disaster.

These affluent people, like this doctor, are fascinating to watch. Have you ever met someone who was so smart, so brilliant, so highly educated, so intellectually "superior" that you found them to be incredibly stupid as people? That was the doctor. She could score like a champ on a Mensa quiz but couldn't figure out common everyday activities. It is like a professor I knew who washed his new Mercedes with a Brillo soap pad. No common sense. No perception of reality. Never liked those sorts of people. Especially when they run our government and are newspaper editors. What is far, far worse, is when you find that many of these people have no moral compass. They are not so much immoral as they are amoral. It is like they have no standards of behavior, that they almost purposely see themselves as too smart, too "enlightened" to behave like the rest of us peasants. But I digress.

Well, in any case, I got the defendant out of jail on bail bond. After securing his release, I took him out to lunch to talk about the case. He did not seem all that concerned about the developments. He asked very few questions and was tight lipped. I did most of the talking. I could not get him to open-up. As an aside, he ordered a dessert, a thick chocolate cake. He was more into that cake than he was in the dire circumstances of his arrest and possible prison sentence. I know this may seem irrelevant and inconsequential, but it seemed odd to me. My background told me that there was more to this than I then knew. As a kid, when I was confronted by the cops, whether it be for cherry bombs in a Brooklyn Street corner or for an assault at a Connecticut restaurant you vent big time. "I didn't do it!" "They did it!" "I was defending myself!" There is nothing worse than being accused of a crime that you did not commit. Nothing.

Now the work begins. After numerous consultations with the client, in every interview, you always ask the question: as to whether they have told you everything there is to know about the matter. Is there anything out there I should know? There is nothing in the world worse for a defense attorney to be surprised in court. Of course, you do all the discovery you can, given that the preliminary hearing discovery is rather limited. You try to leave no stone unturned. Ok, great, time to prepare for the preliminary hearing.

I don't normally waive the preliminary hearing even though the burden of proof is only "probable cause." The reason is that in such serious cases as this you want to hear what evidence the prosecution has in the case, which includes the testimony of the investigative officers and the witnesses, if any. You want to know what is out there and test their credibility. Are they believable?

Sure enough, the defense lawyer's nightmare has begun. I was informed that a search warrant of the doctor's house and the defendant's room was initiated by the Police Department and that I was to see the results of their search. A camera was found in plain sight and in plain view in defendant's room, with undeveloped photos in the camera. The police department developed the photos. The photos were numerous of the nine-year-old in a naked condition, in compromising posed positions in defendant's room and, on defendant's bed. After a review of the warrant, and attached affidavits, I was horrified and shocked! Probably the worst day of my professional career. As you could probably guess, I confronted my client with the photos. It was not pretty. He confessed to me that he did take the photos, etc.

I was extremely upset with the defendant. I yelled and ranted at defendant, "Remember, I told you to tell me everything!!??" "Remember, I told you to not leave anything out or unsaid?!" "Remember??!!" The facts were worse than I ever imagined. What if the client had given me the camera prior to the search warrant? In the early eighties, there were no specific provisions dealing with this issue in the American Bar Association Rules of Professional Responsibility. If my client had given me that camera while seeking my advice the attorney-client privilege would protect the information communicated to me by the client. It follows that if I were given that evidence I would be bound by the attorney-client privilege and must protect the information and the camera given to me by the client, since disclosure would imply a statement. To my mind an exceedingly difficult situation to be in. A lawyer could be disbarred and lose his license if he had betrayed that attorney-client privilege. In any case, that was not what had happened. I was not put in that position.

This was probably the most depressing case I ever had. I now had few options and even fewer defenses at that point. After a long discussion with my client, wherein he had his come to Jesus' moment, we opted for a plea bargain to limit the time to be served, but I wanted a sentencing hearing because of the situation he found himself in with the idiot victim's mother. The sentencing hearing was deeply emotional. I had to limit the damage to the kid. He had no priors, but the facts were hard to deal with. Toward the end of the hearing, the doctor wanted to address the court. This is when the judge's face turned a bright crimson red. The judge reviewed the sentencing report, knew the entire situation, since we had discussed all the facts in chambers and the District Attorney, being a fair man, admitted that the doctor was ill advised in her child rearing skills by allowing the naked nonsense under her roof in front of her nine-year-old daughter.

Knowing that a nutty parent is not a defense to the crime but can be used as a mitigating factor in sentencing, the judge, who was well aware of all the facts presented in the court file, said to the doctor that she had a right to address the court. "But if you do," he said, "I will allow Mr. DiLorenzo to exam you on the record, and I promise you it will not be pretty. I suggest you sit down, stay quiet, and contemplate your lack of parenting skills." She sat down and waived her right to address the court. He was sentenced to some state prison time.

This unfortunate matter was a great example as to how a client's lack of candor can create a snowball effect of unforeseen outcomes. Never, ever lie to your lawyer or fail to tell him everything. Always tell the truth no matter what the truth is. Lying to your doctor or your lawyer can have fatal consequences. There are times when things are not what they seem to be. These are the times when your own background comes in very handy and can clear up the fog. You must use your gut feelings. Finally, as I made abundantly clear, some so-called "intellectuals" are dumb, just plain dumb.

8
Till the Fat Lady Sings

I like a good personal injury case. The liability is clear in many of these cases, the financial rewards are good, and you can get out from under those pesky criminal cases for a while. Here are the facts: My client, 67 years old, married, rather heavy, but a nice lady. She was driving down the street in a city in California when she was hit by a drunk driver who hit her full on in a head on collision. Both cars were totaled, and my client suffered profoundly serious injuries to her legs, hips, thighs. The other driver was also injured but not to the extent of her injuries. What made this case so bizarre and media worthy was the fact that the defendant was an employee of the City as the Chief Traffic Safety Engineer of the City, and had a BAL of .17 plus, and had just come from a party hosted by the City for all traffic safety engineers in the bay area. The city served alcohol, and lots of it, all the beer and wine you could drink. Are you kidding me?! The media jumped all over this case. The newspapers and TV channels sought me out for an interview. Being shy and self-effacing, I did talk to them. I was careful not to say anything that might prejudice my case, but the fact pattern was far too delicious for the media to pass up.

This was an exceedingly difficult case. I mean sure, we receive an admission of liability from the employee and his insurance company, but not from the City. They fought this case tooth and nail. The settlement from the employee did not nearly compensate my client for her injuries. I had to go after the city. The City defended the case on the theory that they had no liability, that they were under dram shop laws, that just because they served all the beer and wine you could drink at a party of traffic safety engineers does not translate into liability. I was stunned by that defense. They offered no settlement. The case had to go to trial. I asked a friend to represent my client's husband on a loss of consortium claim. So, go to trial it did. I must admit the city hired the biggest and best defense firm in the Bay Area and they did a job on us both. The trial took over two weeks to try. The trial judge tried to be fair and did permit an instruction on the negligence of the city in permitting an employee to get drunk while on the job and supplying the alcohol. The jury found for the Defendant City. I was mortified.

This is one of those cases in which it is not how brilliant you are as an attorney, or what ivy league school you came from, but how persistent you are in swimming against the raging river flow, and not surrendering until justice is done. As the saying goes, "It's not over till the fat lady sings." I appealed. The California Court of Appeals in San Jose would not take the case, transferring it to the Appellate Court in Los Angeles. Apparently, the Appellate Court felt it either had a conflict or that it did not want to deal with it for some reason. The Court believed that the matter should best be resolved in Los Angeles. Oh my, the big boys in L.A. I thought I needed help on this one. Big time help. I called that organization "Mothers Against Drunk Driving" or "MADD" for their help and asked them if they would prepare and file an amicus brief. They said they had been following the case and would enter an appearance and file a brief! Excellent.

44

MADD retained a firm In Sacramento, reviewed the record and believed that we were right, and the City was wrong. They filed the amicus brief, and we filed a brief arguing that the city should be held liable under the facts of the case. The day came for the hearing in Los Angeles. We took a plane down to L.A. for the hearing. The Appellate court room was elegant. You could hear our knees knock, since we knew that the justices would be grilling us on the facts and the law. They called the case, I entered our appearance, and started to argue. After only several minutes the lead Justice interrupted me and stated that they knew our position well but wanted to hear from defense counsel. Defense counsel was one of those ivy league law school grads, impeccably dressed (I think it was Armani), a bit arrogant and looked confident. It did not take much time for the court to undress the man. Each Justice took him apart. All the Justices were of one mind in that if the City is to host a party and serve alcohol, they have liability, when these traffic safety engineers drive drunk. One of the Justices admitted he was a recovering alcoholic and was rather emphatic and would not accept that the city could not have known their traffic engineer was intoxicated under the fact pattern, or that people who drink would only drink so much and not drink to excess.

In short, the court reversed. We filed a Motion for Summary Judgment based on the court's opinion. The motion was granted. The trial judge did state that he left that trial with an uneasy feeling in that he should have granted our NOV. (Judgment Notwithstanding the Verdict). The case was set for retrial on the issue of damages. On the day of trial, the presiding judge would not give us a courtroom, and told us to wait in the hall until a courtroom was available. This was the presiding judge's way of telling us to settle the case. We waited for hours, then days. The presiding judge asked us again to be reasonable and settle the case. I asked for "justice." The judge laughed. "It's all dollars and cents," not justice. I will never forget that. However, we did settle the matter. It was a great deal of money, multiple six figures.

This was one of the most instructive cases I ever handled. My client was compensated, but not nearly as much money was given if the client had been aged 35, beautiful and comely. Yes, age and looks are important in valuing a case. It may not seem fair but ask any trial lawyer.

To this day, I am convinced that one of the reasons we lost was the appearance of the Plaintiff. She was in her late sixties, very obese, not particularly good-looking, not well spoken. Every trial lawyer knows it is best to have a young, good-looking person in a personal injury matter. They always get big bucks. The others, well, you do what you can. As an aside, I had a very pretty blonde, blue eyed, young woman as a client who was accidentally shot in her finger by a bar patron. This woman had just completed her modeling portfolio the week before. The man who shot her was creating a disturbance in the bar, and should have been removed by management, but was not. We sued the bar. The defense denied liability, arguing that the bar was not negligent and did not foresee the shooting. After the defense attorneys met the Plaintiff, the insurance carrier wanted nothing to do with the case. It settled for six figures without batting an eyelash. Never went to court. It was one of the quickest settlements I ever had. Doesn't seem fair, does it? It isn't.

If you believe you are right, do not give up or give in. Every person who is injured by the fault of someone else deserves to be fairly compensated no matter who they are or what they look like. They have a life that is every bit as valuable as the most "beautiful' person out there. They too are loved.

9
Leaving the Big City

I have always wanted to live in the country. Coming from South Brooklyn, the slower pace of country life had always attracted me. My Sicilian mother grew up on a farm in New Jersey, and our summer visits to that town were some of the best years of my life. Besides, I grew up with Hopalong Cassidy, Roy Rogers, and John Wayne. The movie "The Searchers" changed my life forever. I wanted a small ranch, horses, you know, cowboy boots. I moved to a small, old, gold mining town in the Sierra foothills of Northern California. Besides, I felt that a small-town atmosphere would have a slower paced legal community. Wow was I wrong.

Being a lawyer in a relatively small county is different. Vastly different. All the lawyers know each other well. You're up against the same lawyers again and again. In these communities, you tread lightly. In the city, you melt into the woodwork. Many lawyers go out of their way to screw you anyway they can. They can't do that in a small town and survive. Do it, and it will come back to bite you. What made the practice so different was the closeness of the legal community. I made friends with every court clerk, bailiff, and as many deputies as I could in the county. My dad once told me "You get far more with honey than with vinegar." The man was right. This is where I part company with many of my colleagues.

I go out of my way to make friends with these employees. When you do so, you have no idea how much easier your job becomes. These good people have done me so many favors; over the years, I have lost count. Many public defenders do the opposite and make enemies with the lawyers in the District Attorney's office, and they all hate law enforcement. How foolish they are. You must make friends with all the court employees, and deputies. In many cases, they are the real power in the courts. Then again, public defenders are different. They wear too much corduroy, Borns, and ill- fitting shirts, looking "frumpy." To them all defendants are "victims." I knew one public defender who always wore hiking boots to court! The top button of his shirt was always lonely. He was chastised by a judge for his appearance .

My relationship with the clerks and deputies became, over the years, quite close. We went on camping trips with them, lunches, dinners, etc. I was even retained by some deputies to represent them in various civil actions, like child custody disputes, will contests, personal injury cases, etc. I never charged a penny for my services, but the gratitude I received was priceless. However, on one occasion, a retired deputy presented me with a gift to show his appreciation. At a dinner in a posh hotel, I was presented with a Colt, Single Action Army Revolver. I mean, Roy Rogers would have been jealous! I was stunned. One of the best gifts I have ever received or will ever receive.

10

Cases They Didn't Teach You About in Law School

1)   The Flying Douche

When you are new in town, you're not as picky as you would be otherwise. You take cases because you either need the money or you need to get your feet wet with the legal system in town. Sometimes you get cases you wish you hadn't. Sometimes you get cases that are so bizarre and so out of the ordinary that you become the butt of way too many laughs. Two of these cases were known as the Flying Douche case and the Please don't flush the Toilet case.   These two cases were given to me by a retiring lawyer. I think he was trying to get rid of them. I should have asked what they were all about before accepting them. I was trying to do this elderly lawyer a favor. No good deed goes unpunished.

I interviewed the client. Here are the facts, as stated in the court files. Mrs. A had a dinner party at her home. After dinner, they all agreed to go to a restaurant for drinks and dessert. Mrs. A went to her bathroom to "freshen up." While in the bathroom she used a disposable douche to do whatever douches are supposed to do. She filled the container with the appropriate liquid, placed the top on, placed it in the appropriate orifice, squeezed the bulb and the top shot out like a rocket into her vagina. She tried to extract the device. But no dice. She opened the door of the bathroom a crack and called her husband. "Oh, honey would you come in here, please." The husband comes into the bathroom. You've got what, stuck were? The husband also tried to extract the device, but still no luck. It would not budge.

With no other sensible or viable options, the couple went to the local hospital emergency room, and told the staff the problem. The hospital staff laughed and did not believe them. They both insisted it was true. By sheer unfortunate dumb luck, the date of the hospital visit was April 1st! The staff thought this was an April fool's joke. They all laughed and said: "good try." However, the couple insisted that the problem was very real. "All right, we will have a doctor take a look", they said. The doctor arrived and sure enough, after being placed in the stirrups, there it was, wedged into parts unknown. The doctor did remove the top and I'm sure that emergency room will never be the same.

The problem is you must go to court to explain the action. In California, all cases are sent to the presiding judge for a case management conference, a determination as to whether the case should be tried, mediated, or sent to a settlement conference. Plaintiff's lawyer must, in public, in front of all the lawyers waiting their turn, describe the case, the facts, and so on. Try describing this products liability case with a straight face. Of course, the court howled with laughter. I did the best I could under the circumstances. "Surely, Mr. DiLorenzo, you can get this case settled" said the presiding judge, giving me 30 days to settle the matter. I told the court that I would do the best I can. The case did settle, thank God. The opposing lawyer did tell me other douches did have rocket propelled tips.

I did have that douche and could not figure out how or why the tip flew off its' supply container. Perhaps my client squeezed it too hard, or whatever. I was not going to dwell on it. However, I did not keep that douche.

2) Please Don't Flush the Toilet

I don't think I would have taken this case on my own. The fact pattern was as peculiar, if not as unusual as the "flying Douche case." However, this elderly lawyer gave me some good cases to finish up, that I could not pass up. Sometimes, you must take the good with the bad.

The complaint and the court file state two friends decided to go to lunch. They both were about 50 plus years of age, except that the plaintiff was a large woman. Some doctors would say morbidly obese. I believe she must have weighed in about 300 plus pounds. The friends eat lunch, talk, and are having a good time. The Plaintiff needs to use the restroom. She does so. She sits on the toilet and the seat breaks in two. I mean, the seat is destroyed. Her butt is shoved into the toilet. She simply could not extricate herself from that toilet, no matter how she tried. Her friend, knowing she had been gone a long time, went to the lady's room to see if she needed any assistance. Her friend then discovered her predicament. She could not get that butt to budge. She called the manager. He could not help as well. That was his story, but I think he wanted no part of it. They called the fire Department.

A fire truck arrived with several firemen. They could not extricate her butt from that toilet as well. From what I recall, it may have been two Firefighters trying to remove the woman from the toilet. The firemen then decided to try another tactic, to break the entire toilet bowl with a sledgehammer. After

51

turning off the water, a fireman wielded that sledgehammer at the bowl and broke it in pieces, freeing the entrapped buttocks. Only then was she free of the water closet. I believe she must have been on that toilet for hours.

So, what's a lawyer to do? Again, I had to describe the facts of the case to the court. More laughter. The judge said: "Mr. DiLorenzo, where do you get these cases?" That case settled as well.

Look, everyone should be treated fairly, no matter what they look like or what physical shape they are in. The lady was obese. But the toilet seat manufacturer, and/or the restaurant owner should anticipate that a heavy person would sit on their toilet seats. It was entirely foreseeable that an old toilet seat would need to be replaced occasionally.

3) Chicken Fever

This case was given to me as a gift wrapped by the County. Sometimes when you have practiced long enough, and the judges are a bit overworked, they assign certain cases to experienced lawyers to act as a pro-tem judge (temporary judge) on certain matters. And sometimes if a judge is not particularly fond of you, they also assign troublesome cases for you to act as pro-tem. I believe that is what happened to me in this matter.

At the time, I was living on my ranch where we raised and bred horses. There were times when in court colleagues would be brushing my suit jacket of alfalfa just before the morning calendar. I could really relate to Oliver Douglas from that old sitcom, Green Acres. It was no secret what my interests were, and it was no secret that I practiced law in the big city, San Francisco. This case came before the court via the Board of Supervisors wherein a new couple who had moved from San Francisco to our little rural county to "get away from it all." They were seemingly a nice couple. They were typical, yuppie-affluent, city "Dinks," double or dual income, no kids. But they had this ongoing dispute with their neighbors. Their neighbors owned a few acres in an unincorporated part of the county and raised chickens for their eggs. They consumed and sold them at the farmer's market. Every morning like clockwork, the roosters would crow and wake up these city folk neighbors. They also complained about the odor of the chickens. They complained to the Sheriff's Department to no avail, then made a complaint to the Board of Supervisors. The Board then referred the matter to the court, in which the court referred the matter to me to conduct a hearing on the complaint.

I don't know much about chickens, but the Court thought the case was perfect for me. Hmmm. So, I agreed to hear the case. The two parties sat on opposite sides of the bench. One party was rather yuppie looking, with Coach and Dolce & Gabbana apparel. The other party was...rather earthy looking. More like Ma and Pa Kettle, than not. We took some testimony from both. The two sides were not getting along very well. The city folks testified that the rooster crows too early in the morning and his coop mates smelled bad. Ma and Pa testified that they had had these chickens for years and never had a problem with anyone before. That is, until the city-folks moved in.

I could see what the problem was right off. The City Folks were just not used to living in the country with all it encompasses. Of course, you're going to have neighbors with chickens, or cows, horses, pigs and what not. I tried to explain that this was a rural county with a county ordinance that gives land-owners in the unincorporated parts of the county a right to farm. This right to farm was a reality in the county and they should have been aware of it. The city folks were not happy, but I think they learned an important lesson. City values are not country values. These conflicts with values are rather common when you move from urban to country life.

Only when the urbanites move in masse to the outlying country areas to create suburbs do values change. Then these people find that they created the very confusion that they tried to get away from.

4)   BTO

Sometimes you get a divorce matter where neither side will listen to any reason or rationalization. This should have been one of the easiest divorces since this was a short- term marriage of only two years, there were no children, and the property was not much to talk about. The husband could have easily done a do-it-yourself divorce since there were little in the way of issues. But what the wife did to her husband was unforgivable. It could never be forgiven. She took his Bachman-Turner, Overdrive album, and refused to return it!!

I know it sounds petty, could even be thought of as a peddle or paltry an issue. But not to my client. He wanted that BTO album by hook or by crook; and he wanted it now. I asked him the obvious, "go buy another BTO album." His face became red with anger and enraged. "No!" "No!" "I want that album." He informed me he had had that album for years, played it all the time. It seemed to me that my client had some sort of cosmic connection with it. He wanted that album, and I could not talk him out of it. I spent several weeks trying to convince the ex-wife to give him that record album back, but she would not budge. Finally, she agreed to give it back, but he had to pay for it by giving her something in return.

Sometimes you find yourself spending a great deal of time doing things that seem to be so peevish and small. But to others they are the world. I have learned to just go with it. Perhaps that record album had more value to him than could be readily seen. Some lawyers would view such people with such issues as beneath them and not worthy of their time. But in the real world, grunt lawyers know it is what it is.

5)   Pigs in a Blanket

This was a different, rather unique divorce case. There were no children of this marriage and the marital property they held did not seem to be extensive.

Whenever I interview a client about a divorce, I feel obligated to ask if the marriage can be saved. And if it can, perhaps a legal separation would be in the offing. Then the parties can go to counseling until such time as the marriage can be patched up and reunite or agree to a permanent separation or divorce as the only option.

I was representing the wife in this divorce and since this was a long -term marriage of over 14 years, I asked what the problem was. She said: "it's my pigs."

"It's your what," I asked? "My pigs."   I asked her if they both raise pigs. She said, no, "only I raise the pigs." "I don't understand. So, what is wrong with your pigs?" I asked her. She told me that she loves those pigs, but that her husband hates them. I asked what kind of pigs do you have and how many? She told me she had five pigs and that they were all Pot Belly Pigs. I inquired if the two of them could negotiate a sort of accommodation with those pigs. She said she tried but that the problem is that one of them likes to sleep in the bed with them. She said the problem is "Oliver." Who's "Oliver?" "Oliver is my pet pig."   "Oliver" will not sleep anywhere other than their bed.

I told her there may be a problem here. She began to tell me how intelligent they were. She stated that "Oliver" was the dominant pig and rather territorial and would not give up their bed. I must admit, I did not know what to say about this. I know nothing about pigs, and it was clear to me that my client would not under any circumstances give up "Oliver," the pig. So, a divorce was the only way to go.

All the paperwork was prepared and after the jurisdictional time limit, we went to court for the final divorce decree. In court, I met the husband for the first time. He was a scraggly man, looked like the type that would not mind having "Oliver" in bed with the two of them. Anyway, after we asked my client the jurisdictional questions, and the court approved the final decree, the husband wanted to say something to the court. I hate it when that happens. He stood and railed against his now ex-wife as to what he had to put up with that pig. He then said, "the pig under the blankets was the last straw," and that "one pig in the bed was enough." He then said, "I waited a long time to say that." The judge admonished the man over his statement.

After the case was over, I was called into the judge's chambers over another matter that was on the calendar. The judge and several other lawyers were laughing over the pig case. The judge did say something to the effect that only I would have a pig case before the court. Well, it is what it is. But I do dislike any client, mine, or someone else's, who insists on addressing the court without prior knowledge. You never know what they will say, or whether they will embarrass you or the court.

11

State vs. 'Nam Vet,' Round One

Sometimes you get a case that makes your reputation in the community. Sometimes a lawyer wants a case that is so notorious, with such media attention, that his name is all over the newspapers, radio and sometimes TV. This was one of those cases. We all heard that a man, a Vietnam veteran, walked into the Sheriff's Department with a rifle and shot up the ceiling and upper walls. He did what!? What was this all about? That kind of thing just did not happen in the foothills.

I did not seek the case, but the veteran's wife called me and retained my services. Here are the facts: The 'Nam vet was about 35 years old, a combat veteran from Vietnam. He had no priors. However, he had some self-protective tendencies when confronted with certain stimuli because of the war. As he described it to me, the odor of diesel fuel would tweak him and send him into a panic, or any kind of swamp would do it. The court file alleges that my client went to the Sheriff's office to turn in a rifle. He did not trust himself with it. When he walked into the office with the rifle, there was no one there. A women deputy suddenly walked in, surprised him, and he reacted by shooting the rifle, spraying the walls, and ceiling with several bullets. Three deputies ran into the office, tackled, and cuffed him. He was charged with attempted murder, assault with a deadly weapon, etc.

He had sat in jail for several days when I was retained. He was in jail since no bail had been set. I asked for a bail hearing. This case was all over the news media. The foothills are known for being peaceful places with little crime. So, media attention was inevitable. Every time there was a hearing, the press would be there with cameras and reporters. On the day of the bail hearing the judge, a crusty old guy with many years on the bench, heard my argument then promptly refused bail. Look, I have had judges refuse bail before, but it was what he said on the record that infuriated me. He said: "any man who shoots up the Sheriff's office deserves to go to state prison!"

Are you kidding me! The judge said that on the record! How in hell am I supposed to get a fair trial in this county or anywhere else. I left the court room in a huff. My temper flared. Of course, the reporters followed me and asked for comments. I was ready for them, but never say anything to reporters when you are angry and hot under the collar. I said to the reporters that what the judge said was out of line, outrageous, and that there would be "no justice in this judges' courtroom today." Oops. A good lawyer should always bridle his tongue. However, there are times when you just can't help yourself. The following week at yet another bail hearing the judge gave me the bail, but used that opportunity to scalp, fray, and skin me alive for what I had said to the press and did so in public. Of course, the press printed it all. Nice.

The press can be your best friend or your worst enemy. They can make or break your case. When you must talk to the press never promise more than you can produce. Be factual and always keep your client's best interests in mind, not your own. Far too many lawyers get into the publicity trap. They see publicity as a means of becoming famous, or infamous, as it were. It becomes a problem when too much publicity gives your client no chance to have a fair trial. Then you have problems.

This public tar and feathering were not unnoticed by many. The District Attorney and a friend, the chief probation officer, knowing that what I said was not entirely out of line, wanted a meeting with the judge to patch up the relationship. We all met wherein the judge tried to tell me he was also in combat, in WW2, was also traumatized by it, but that he never shot up a sheriff's office. He was apparently not sympathetic to combat veterans with problems, and believed PTSD was an excuse. We patched up our differences. I told the court I was going to file a motion to amend the plea to not guilty by reason of insanity, and for a mental exam of the defendant, since the man needed a complete evaluation regarding post-traumatic stress.

The District Attorney agreed. I found that the best Veterans Administration facility that dealt with PTSD was in Menlo Park, California. I contacted them and they sent the best PTSD man there to evaluate the veteran. After a thorough evaluation, it was determined that he had "one of the worst cases of PTSD the VA had seen." After a lengthy discussion of the matter with the District Attorney, we all agreed to send the Vet to the Menlo Park Veteran's Administration Hospital for inpatient treatment. That was it. The matter was later resolved with a plea, no jail time. The veteran only had inpatient treatment for as long as the VA deemed necessary. He was at that VA hospital for six months. A good result. This incident could have been disastrous for that Vet.

I have an enormous respect for veterans, especially those who have experienced combat. Post-traumatic Stress Syndrome is real, make no mistake. These men and women suffer plenty. During those jail house visits, he told me stories of combat; of the faces of men and women he had conflict with in 'Nam and in which he will never forget. Far too many of

59

them commit suicide and I believe they need all the help the VA and private industry can muster. I include lawyers who should be on that line to help, whether the Vet can afford their help or not. As a footnote that crusty old judge referred many public defenders conflict cases to me. Sometimes when you stick to your principles you earn respect.

12
The Pillsbury Dough Boy Case

If you're wondering where I get the names of these cases, It's not me. It was either the media, the press, the bailiffs, or the court clerks that give these unofficial tongue-in-cheek names to cases. The court employees deal with these cases every day and they naturally give names for I.D. purposes and for a chuckle. In the courts, you take a chuckle wherever you can find it.

Anyway, let me give you the facts alleged in the court file. A young man, early twenties had some medical and emotional problems. He took some medication that had side effects that made him appear almost perfectly round. He looked like a beach ball with arms and legs. He suffered from severe depression, among other things, and was not taking his medications, since he insisted did not help. He wanted to die. However, he did not have the courage to kill himself. But he thought of a way. He took a shotgun and started shooting out the door of his home. A neighbor called the police. Several cop cars showed up to assess the situation. The defendant started shooting at the patrol cars, hitting their headlights. The standoff eventually ended. The man was arrested and placed in custody. He was charged with attempted murder, assault with a deadly weapon, and others.

The defendant's aunt called and retained me. "Help him as best you can. He has not been well. He has been depressed and wants to die." In these cases, you must get a full medical and psychological work up. You must know what is going on with the guy. We found he had been under medical care but was not taking his medication on a regular basis, and what he was prescribed did not seem to help. The District Attorney's office did not care a wit as to what his problems were, they just wanted him gone, and gone for a long, long time. The wanted those charges of attempted murder, assault with a deadly weapon to stick and wanted a plea. The Deputy District Attorney on the case was a friend of mine, (who later was an usher at my wedding). But hey, business is business. He wanted 7 years in state prison. Not if I can help it! I believed that there was far more to the case than could be seen on the surface.

I knew this case to be a loser. He was not taking his medication. He goes into a tirade. He shoots at the officers, albeit with no intention to kill them, but one shotgun pellet did hit an officer's boot. One must understand that the trial is to take place in a rural, conservative, law-and-order county. Not the best venue for this type of case. It was not San Francisco. However, I decided to take the matter to trial anyway. I had no choice since the DA's office would not deal. I believed my client needed far more than a sentencing hearing. I needed a full- blown display as to this man's situation, his life, his problems both personal and medical, everything there was to know. The only way was a jury trial to show all the facts and circumstances the defendant faced. I believed my only defense was that this incident was a suicide attempt.

Off to trial we go. I knew this Judge. He was a very thoughtful, analytical, and kind man. I felt in my bones that he

62

would understand. Knowing your judges is a vital part of how you proceed in your cases. Some judges are simply so happy and willing to put your client in prison, others not so. If possible, stay away from the former and try to wiggle your way to secure the latter. The trial lasted about a week. The DA put in all kinds of evidence, including the boot with a slightly visible shotgun pellet scrape, the officer's telling the jury they were afraid for their lives (yeah, right! They tend to exaggerate). Went it came to my turn I put on a dog and pony show, a virtual "This is your Life" scenario.

After the closing arguments, the jury deliberated. Of course, my client was found guilty. This is not a big city where jurors have a crying towel. The smaller the community, the more difficult it is to gain an acquittal. The case was set for a sentencing hearing. I asked for half a day. The DA's office insisted on those seven years prison time. I knew the probation officer and gave him all the information I had on my client, including all medical and psychiatric information. After the documentary and witness evidence was admitted, and we made our arguments, the Judge had to make a ruling and sentence my client. The judge said something I will never forget. "Well Mr. DiLorenzo, you lost the battle, but you won the war." The Judge, because of the defendant's maladies of which were so abundantly displayed at trial, refused to send him to prison. He put the man on supervised probation with credit for time served with stringent conditions of probation, including regular visits to his medical doctors, maintenance of his medications, etc. He did very well after that with no further problems. Success!

This case was one of the most instructive cases I had. There are times when a sentencing hearing is simply not enough to get the facts before the court. The courts just will not give you enough time at the hearing to tell the entire story as to why your client did what he did. The judge readily admitted that the trial, with all the witnesses and documents presented, convinced him that my client needed help, not incarceration. My client's act with that shotgun was one of pure desperation for help.

He could not get it otherwise. Sometimes a good lawyer must put himself in the shoes of his client. It should be noted that these go-to-trial decisions can be very risky. The plea bargain is usually far more favorable than what could happen at trial if your client is convicted. But when the DA will not bargain and will not let up you have no choice and no option but to roll the dice. At that point there is nothing to lose. You tell your story and hope for the best. This works well when you have a sympathetic client. Not when you represent a dirt bag.

There is one anecdote I would like to impart as to this case. The bailiff and I knew each other well. We had so many cases with each other that we became buddies. He loved to play practical jokes. His only failing. He was the bailiff in the trial and in the middle, while listening to the officer's testimony, I could see him at his desk reading his usual golf magazine. He had the magazine off his desk high up enough that no one could see him except me. He looks at me with a grin and flips me off in the middle of testimony! I could not contain myself and started to chuckle! The Judge noticed and asked me what was so amusing as to the officers' testimony? What am I going to say? Your bailiff just flipped me the bird? I couldn't do that. No way. I swallowed it whole, apologized, and the trial continued.

Two years later I was invited to the wedding of a lawyer friend. At the reception I was assigned a seat next to that Judge and his wife. On the other side of me the bailiff and his wife were seated. Ok, I got you. I started a conversation with the Judge and asked him; "do you remember a couple years ago when I chuckled in the middle of that jury trial?" "Yes," he said, "I do remember." Now I am going to tell you why I laughed. The bailiff grimaced. "Your bailiff flipped me off with a grin and I couldn't help but chuckle." The Judge sat there quietly for a moment and said in his usual stoic manner "if my bailiff flipped you off, he must have had a very good reason."

13
The Fatal Attraction Case

This was a fascinating case that hit the media big time. Every court appearance held media attention, the TV news sent film crews and reporters to gauge the happenings. It was a reality show before we had reality shows. What made it so tantalizing was the fact that it involved two of the most prominent families in two separate, but neighboring counties. Both families were successful, multi-generational, gold country families involved in similar, if not, competing businesses. Of course, being shy and retiring, I took the case.

The court file alleges the following acts: This case involved the relationship between a couple, both in their twenties, each from those prominent families in neighboring counties. They have this torrid love affair keeping it secret from the families. Now things get dicey. The woman is married to a truly kind and gentle man who is none the wiser. The woman becomes pregnant by the boyfriend. She wants to divorce her husband and get married to this other guy. She wants a child. The man says that this pregnancy is at the wrong time, especially under the circumstances, that they must be more considerate of the families and do things in a more measured manner. He convinces her to seek an abortion. After the abortion, he says, they will continue with the relationship, get married and do things the "right" way. She does not want to do this, but she is in love, and she is talked into an abortion. She does so. Afterward, and predictably, the man cuts off the relationship and wants nothing more to do with her.

As the court file alleges, the woman is incensed, I mean a serious conniption fit. Hell, fire, and brimstone is a woman scorned. Sometime later, late at night, she travels the distance to the neighboring county to the apartment of her former lover. She is carrying a semi-automatic pistol. She gains entry to the apartment and while he is sleeping, she sits at the end of his bed with pistol in hand. He awakens to the muzzle end of a pistol and an embittered, women. She tells him he is going to die and afterward will kill herself. This goes on for some time. After enduring this lengthy lecture of his impending death, he jumps up and makes a lightening quick exit out the window of this apartment to the parking lot. The startled woman jumps up, and chases him down the parking lot, firing the pistol at him repeatedly. It was later determined that she fired that pistol at least six times.

I am retained by the women's mother. The father did not like me much because I stepped on his toes in another matter. The woman is charged with attempted murder, assault with a deadly weapon, felony false imprisonment, etc. This case is going to take a bit of creativity. After viewing the scene, and gathering all the facts, I did not believe she was trying to kill the man, I believe she was acting out her anger, and grieving for the loss of her future with this creep. If she was trying to kill him then why were the bullet holes high up in the parking garage roof, instead of in the walls?

Now, this case is in the jurisdiction of a county northwest of my home county. I have spent some time in that county on other matters but not a great deal of time. After a cursory investigation, I find that the creepy guy's father is one of the most successful lawyers in that county, is very well known, and influential. Sometime prior to the preliminary hearing, I inquire as to the prelim judge's relationship with the "victim's" father. The Judge states he knows the father, but not well and has no conflict or bias. Ok, I did my job. He then states that he now has a conflict and a bias against, not my client, but me for even asking that question! The Judge is angry at me! I'm trying to do my job investigating all aspects of the case to assure my client receives a fair trial and this guy is insulted!? Stop it. He should have known better than to attack my motives.

On the morning of the preliminary hearing, I walk into the courtroom, and it is filled with people, reporters, cameras, deputies, clerks, etc. To explain, a preliminary hearing is not a trial but a probable cause hearing to determine whether the is sufficient evidence to determine that the defendant "probably" did commit the crimes charged. Such hearings are rather loose, hearsay evidence is admissible, the strict rules of evidence are not observed. Many lawyers do not like prelims since their clients are bound over to the Superior Court for trial in 99% of the cases. They usually waive these Preliminary Hearings. I like to use them to test out the prosecutor, to see what they have and possibly strike a count or two.

At the hearing there was testimony from the boyfriend as to what my client did to him, the entry to his apartment, pointing the pistol at him, blah, blah, blah. I had my turn at the cross-examination. I asked him some questions as to the relationship, the numerous sexual encounters with a married woman, the promises of marriage, and so on. I then asked him about the fact that he got her pregnant and his insistence on an abortion. When that came out, the audience gasped, and my client's mother screamed! The mom was totally unaware. The media got what they wanted — a reality show.

I got what I wanted. The victim was now the bad guy here, not the defendant.

Now comes the footwork, the legal research, the investigation, the preparation of witnesses. I hire a private investigator to search for anything I can use against the "victim." He finds it. This guy is dealing in illicit drugs, including performance enhancing drugs. A break- through. Did the use of such drugs affect his memory as to the incident? Did the drugs cause the man to possibly exaggerate the facts of the incident? I subpoenaed the man's mother, his lawyer father, his grandmother, anyone connected with this guy. I consulted with experts.

The day of trial comes. We entered a filled courtroom with prospective jurors, media people, etc. The Judge enters the court room. "The defense is ready your honor." Silence from the District Attorney. The Superior Court Judge looks at the District Attorney, states that he wishes to see counsel in chambers. In chambers, I get the feeling that something is up. The Judge states that this case has gotten out of hand, too much publicity with too many lives affected. The District Attorney agrees. The DA wants to drop the attempted murder charge, the aggravated assault and have my client plead to a simple false imprisonment charge!

Oh my. I must have hit a nerve. I told the DA that I did not want my client to go to prison or jail on any charge. The DA promptly said: "no jail time, just credit for time served." It was explained to me that the victim's family liked my client, realized she had been through a lot with the pregnancy, the abortion, the rejection by their son, and wanted the case to simply go away. In other words, the victims' family reputation was at stake, and they would do anything to save it including twisting the DA's arm with a plea to the judge. "I will have to discuss this with my client," I said.

I discussed the offer with my client and client's mother, the matriarch of the family. Mom was delighted and gave me a hug. The client not so much. I think she was just bitter over the whole scenario. She wanted the boyfriend to be exposed for the creep that he was. In any case, the client agreed with the plea deal. Her life was saved.

I probably took this matter too personally. I felt for this woman and her mom. I thought her act of shooting that pistol in the air was instructive to me as to how she was feeling, how hurt she was, how her emotions had gone out of control. The boyfriend was bad. He was a user. She never wanted that abortion. She did it as the only way she could keep him. Yes, she committed adultery. Her husband was as much the victim as my client. To prevail, I had to use as much creativity as I could think of. My gut told me the family did not want this trial to go forward. I was right. As an aside, the client and her husband reconciled and are doing well.

14
Hollywood vs The Hillbilly Neighbors

This case came to me from a recommendation from a former client. This new client was wealthy. He was a Hollywood star, and has been in a lot of movies, including Patton, El Dorado, etc. He knew all the big stars, John Wayne, George C. Scott, etc. I liked hearing stories about them, and he liked telling me. This man had a rather pushy temperament. He had this sense of entitlement and was quite used to having his way. He was brash, hard drinking, and would not take "no" for an answer. He was border line narcissistic, not sociopathic. What makes this case so problematic was not so much the issues involved. It was a simple road easement case and the responsibility for the maintenance of the road. A rather common problem in more rural areas. Usually, these cases settle with a compromise as to who is responsible for what.

The problem was the personalities involved. My client owned a large quarter horse ranch, big house, beautiful barns, caretakers, the whole nine yards. I know horses and he had some exceptionally fine animals. He wanted everything done his way, without question. However, he wanted everything done his way by the neighbors as well. My client wanted all contiguous roads groomed, widened, and looking pretty at the expense of all who used the roads. The neighbors said no way. There was a great deal of anger and resentment from the neighbors, so much so that my client believed his horses were in danger of being shot by one of these neighbors. My client did not know how to use that honey rather than vinegar to get what he wanted. He caused a great deal of animosity by all on that road.

We sued several neighbors on the issue of rights of way, easements, and maintenance. No one would settle, and I sure tried. The case went to trial for 5 days. We had witnesses, exhibits, maps, the whole bag of tricks. My client, while I am making a pitch to the court on an issue of evidence, looks at the opposing counsel and flips him off! The opposing counsel had a come-apart. Opposing counsel stands up, tells the judge that my Hollywood client flipped him the bird, in no uncertain terms. The Judge asked me if I saw it. "No, I didn't see it, your honor." The judge asks the bailiff, "no, I didn't see it either." The Judge admonished my client. Later, in private, I asked my client if he indeed gave opposing counsel the bird. He laughs and says, "most certainly." I implored him to never do such a thing, again. The last thing I needed was a judge having ill feelings for my client.

The end of the trial came, and the Judge had already made his decision. He made a long and philosophical explanation as to his decision on the bench. In short, we won on all issues, and won it all completely! At that point, my client stands up and asks to address the court. Oh no, not a monologue! I rarely ever have good experiences when clients want to address the court without my knowing what they wish to say. But my client insisted. Mr. Hollywood stands up and states that he will give the Defendant's, all his neighbor's, all they have asked for in this suit, lock, stock, and barrel! He then looks at me extends his arms and states: "I just wanted to win!" "Rob," he says, "you did a good job for me but give them what they want." I am in shock, the judge was stunned, and the opposing counsel was uncharacteristically silent. My client was as good as his word. He simply wanted to teach his "backward" neighbors an expensive lesson. The court was not so happy. The judge thought the court was used for my client's purposes to punish the defendants. But the judge let it go since everyone seemed to be happy.

15
Family Values

This is one of those cases that gave you heartburn. Some clients are just not cooperative and easy to deal with. The facts. My client was in his 40's, came from a good family with a high income. His parents owned and operated a large and successful business in a small rural town. The family was well known and liked. This client was married to a good-looking woman with several kids, most in high school in this rural town. So, what's the problem?

The problem, as stated in numerous court files, alleges that my client simply had a drug addiction that he could not shake off. I mean big time. He could not keep his hands off the drugs, all kinds of drugs, meth, cocaine, you name it. By the time his family came to me, he had six prior convictions. The cops busted a drug dealer's residence at 2:00 am. Sure enough, there was my client, inside the residence in a drug stupor, totally out of it. He was arrested for possession, possession for sale, and under the influence. Again, the drug bust was all over the local newspapers, to the humiliation of his wife and high school kids. Can you imagine being in high school and your dad gets arrested and jailed for drug charges, yet again. The kids deserved better from their dad.

This time the DA's office wanted prison time. They were fed up with him and did not want to deal with this nonsense over, and over again. The system can be forgiving for the first time and even a second or third relapse, but, after that the system becomes impatient, even nasty. They believe that when you take up too much of their time and refuse to reform, they figure you're a loser and will not conform your conduct to lawful standards.

I kept hearing on the news that some politicians are complaining that the prisons are filled with marijuana use and possession convictions. In all my years of practice, I have never known that to be true in both California and Wyoming. The courts are quite lenient with use and possession charges and very few spend any time behind bars. Most courts I know are far more apt to accept inpatient or outpatient treatment as a remedy. It happens all the time. The only problems I have had is when the client is on his third, fourth, fifth, even sixth conviction. Then things get dicey. Insofar as the media and politicians who claim that illicit drugs and their use and possession are victimless crimes, they should meet the family of my client.

The wife and family pleaded with me to take the case and get him off, or at least a best-case scenario. However, after six convictions, no promises. It seemed to me that his drug days were over. That he must reform or go to prison. He had reached a point in his life that for the sake of his wife and kids he had to get clean. The client promised to get clean. His position was, in no uncertain terms, that he would do whatever it took to clean up and reform, including inpatient, outpatient care, whatever it took. I told him that after all the prior convictions, no promises, I would try to get the best deal I could and get him on the road to recovery. Some state prison time seemed a certainty in his case.

75

I had long discussions with the DA on this. No way, they wanted prison time, and a good amount of prison time. After the third visit with the DA they suggested my client turn States evidence and give them information on the drug dealers in the county. The District Attorney's office often asks defendants to do this as a means of cleaning up the county, and as a means to show the State a client's reform. But that's not something you ask a client to do unless you have no other way out, not the situation here.

We spent a long time with this case, trying to work out a solution to this man's drug problem so that this would be the last time he would be before the court. I thought of a solution. In California, we have what is called the California Rehabilitation Center, or CRC. I worked out an arrangement where, instead of prison time of several years, my client would spend six months at CRC, then be released under supervised probation. I thought it was a good deal. It limited the amount of time away from the family, he would get the inpatient treatment that he so desperately needed and then be on the road to a full recovery.

I told my client the deal I worked out for him. However most clients do not like CRC. Like so many others, they don't like that CRC would have a seven-year tale on him. That for seven years the police would be stopping him on the street, making house calls, checking on him, testing him, and basically harassing him. In my view, so what. Many clients tell you that they want to be clean for their own sake and for the sake of their kids and family. CRC would help you do that. Unless, of course, the client is giving you a line of nonsense and has no intention of getting clean.

With all the many drug cases I have done, it never fails to amaze me how self-destructive people can be, how so much of their money can be wasted on lawyers, fines, treatments that could be used on far more profitable enterprises.

This man wanted to get clean. But it is very hard for some addicts. Some do not want to pay the price of reformation, of living a clean life. He wanted to get clean. In my experience many want to get clean but on their terms. As always, in these cases, the drug addict's terms meant no rehabilitation and continued relapses. That's exactly why my client had six prior convictions. God knows what was said at home behind closed doors with his wife, mother, father, and high school kids. In my view, there was no other alternative unless he wanted to go to prison. Some would rather go to prison, rather than have that seven-year tail. At least when he got out, there would not be that tail. Look, I tell all my clients they have choices. If you want, I will tell the DA that we did not have a deal. No, my client accepted the deal.

The sentencing hearing was one of my most memorable hearings. The Judge explained and put on record the plea deal and stated that he was not quite in favor of the deal, was reluctant, but that both counsels spent a lot of time hammering out a disposition and would accept it. As usual after all that was said, the Judge asked if defendant had anything to say. The defendant said he would like to address the court. Oh No! I started to panic. Everything your client states in court is on record! This is a point in which the defense counsel has no control!

Defendant stood up and said to the effect that: "This is all unfair. I was at a man's house to buy a car, the cops busted in and arrested everyone including me, ...!" The Judge's face became red as a beet, he stood up from his chair, leaned over the bench and just simply lost it. He yelled at the defendant. "You were there to purchase a car??!!! "Do I look stupid to you!!!" "You, Mr. ------- were found at that house at 2:00 am, in a known drug dealer's house, laid out in a corner of a room, stoned out of your mind and you have the nerve to tell this court that you were there to buy a car!!! The only reason I have consented to this deal was because of your counsel, and ...!!!"

I had never seen a judge so incensed, so outraged. Grabbing at my client's shirt tails, I kept trying to get my client to sit down, but he didn't. He finally sat down, and the Judge kept going after him. After all his prior convictions, the Judge had had enough with this man. Sometimes, not often, even a good judge will simply lose his temper and become unglued. He certainly did that day.

After serving his six months, my client remained clean for as far as I am aware.

16
State vs 'Nam Vet,' Round Two

When your practice has an emphasis on criminal defense, repeat business becomes a way of life. Sure, repeat business is great when you own a hardware store, but sometimes in criminal law practice it becomes worrisome. Is the client a habitual offender? I take my client's welfare quite seriously. I try to counsel them to take the right path and be productive in life and in the community. I can be accused of giving my clients dreary lectures.

This case came as a great surprise to me. The defendant was the veteran who suffered from PTSD, who shot up the Sheriff's office several years before, described in Chapter Eleven. Except this time, he was charged with second degree murder! I was retained yet a second time. His wife came to my office and again prevailed upon me to take on his defense yet again. I knew this guy and for him to kill someone he must have been presented with one hell of a provocation. Sure enough, I was right.

If one thought the pre-trial publicity in the prior matter was big, it was nothing compared to this case. Homicide in small rural communities does not happen very often. This community had not seen one for years. So, the publicity was huge, yet again. I was a great deal smarter about it and more calculated with the press than previously. I never went out of my way to contact the press but when they contacted me, I placed my client as the victim in the matter. It was my veteran that was home, minding his own business, and it was the deceased that was the antagonist.

The facts are simple. It was the fourth of July holiday. And the town was filled with tourists, and especially bikers from biker gangs. One of the bikers was told about Mr. ...... and was told that he was a "tough dude." The drunk biker wanted to see how tough this guy was. (That was my version, DA said otherwise). He found out where he was living and approached his house. Please understand that the biker was all decked out in a sleeveless shirt, multiple biker tattoos, had been drinking heavily, and was wearing a sheathed knife.

My client was home and saw this strange, unknown, obviously drunk, man climbing the stairs to his house. He presented the biker with a loaded 30-30 Winchester carbine and told him not to go any further. The biker kept climbing those stairs. My client cocked the lever. The man kept moving closer. My client shot the biker dead on the stairway.

My client was charged with second degree murder. Again, the case got plenty of media attention. This time the DA's office was out for blood. They wanted him gone, in prison, not to see the light of day ever again. What was disturbing to me was how far the DA's office was willing to go to see my client burn. There was a vengeance to be displayed by that office that surprised even me. To give you an example, the defendant was arrested at his home, handcuffed, and placed into the back seat of a police cruiser. The veteran was Mirandized and asked all kinds of questions. As is all too common in these cases, the defendant started talking and everything he said was being taped. With a cursory investigation I knew about the existence of that tape. I asked the chief deputy DA for a copy of that tape. He told me that he would give it to me, but that it would do me no good since the tape was incomprehensible, garbled, and of no use to anyone. Ok. I was suspicious. Always suspect an impropriety about "garbled tapes."

At the preliminary hearing, the Chief Deputy DA presents the tape! I came unglued! I jumped up and objected to the attempted admission of the tape since my copy was refused and I was specifically told it was unavailable because of it being useless. In fact, the Deputy DA and I had a shouting match in court over that tape. The shouting was loud, fast, and furious. The Judge kept shouting at us both to quiet down and that he wanted to see us both in chambers, NOW! In chambers, the Judge simply asked the Chief Deputy DA if, in fact, did Mr. DiLorenzo ask for the tape? The Chief Deputy DA said, yes, he did, but...That was it! The Judge got noticeably angry and told the Chief Deputy DA that he would not admit that tape into evidence. He then, with a degree of scorn, scolded the Chief Deputy DA, about his unprofessional conduct. Sometime prosecutors will try to get some things past you, and will, if you let them. It's your job not to let them get past you. Don't ever think prosecutors are always even handed and fair. They are not. They love to win, too.

The defendant is bound over for trial. What to do now. The DA's office would not relent, not this time. They believed that the defendant was dangerous and had to be put away. I saw it differently. I saw a man who owned a home and was presented with a biker who was trying to gain entry into his home. The DA did not see self-defense in this case since the knife was still safely sheathed in its holder at the time of his death, since there was no immediate threat of death or serious bodily harm. I saw it differently in that the defendant need not wait until the knife was presented to him to defend himself. After all, defendant did warn the biker. In addition, I knew the fact that the veteran had a gun in his possession was a big deficit. His prior conviction had probation terms that precluded possession of a firearm. I had no defense to that count. At times like this whether you go to trial or not must depend on the client and what he wants to do. All you can really do is give your client your best advice, tell him all the options, and let him make the decision. My client asked if the charge could be dropped to manslaughter, with a minimum 2-year sentence. With time served he would be out in a year. Not likely, I said, the DA's office was set in concrete.

It has been my experience, sometimes when a case is around a long enough time, is in court for this motion, that motion, when the media has gotten a hold of it, that the State gets a bit antsy and wants to deal, especially when it may seem iffy if they would even get a conviction. I kept shouting to the court, and the media "self-defense!" A short time before trial, after yet another hearing on the matter, the Chief Deputy DA shouts at me if I would take a manslaughter deal. "Well, I don't know," I said. I'll think about it and consult with my client.

I felt good about a trial in this matter. Defendant's PTSD was a factor, the biker was an unattractive victim, and was the antagonist in the situation that was presented to defendant, who was peacefully in his home. We could defend this. However, my client had a firearm he was not permitted to have, was not particularly an attractive client, had a checkered past, the kind of client you do not want to take the stand and testify. This rural community was not San Francisco. You always have that law-and-order community attitude to think about when making such determinations.

However, I left it to my client. I told him at worst, manslaughter has a two, four, and six-year term. If you take the deal, they will want a six-year term, plus a consecutive term for owning a firearm which was a violation of probation on his first offense. I told the defendant that I would not agree to any term but would simply request an extensive sentencing hearing. My client opted for the manslaughter conviction with the sentencing hearing.

The day came for the sentencing hearing, and we put on a hell of a 3-ring circus. The Chief Deputy DA decided not to appear but sent his senior deputy. He didn't like me anymore! The wife, neighbors, doctors, testified along with the evidence admitted including medical records, and so on. I argued strenuously for the two-year term, knowing that if he received that term, as stated, with credit for time served he would be out in less than a year! While I argued, I was repeatedly interrupted by the Senior Deputy DA. The hearing was very antagonistic and combative. Then the Senior Deputy said something remarkably stupid. He told the court that every time Mr. DiLorenzo says something the court listens and takes it to heart. Every time we say something, the court doesn't listen and dismisses it. He also said, it would not surprise me if this court gave this man only a two- year term for killing a man!!

The Judge became quite angry at the man's tone and his statement. His face turned a crimson shade. The Judge said: "Ok Mr. .... that is what I'm going to do!" My client received two years only for the manslaughter and firearm possession charge to run concurrently, with credit for time served! We saw this as a great victory. He was out in less than a year. My only regret was what if my client was not who he was, with that prior situation under his belt, would the DA's office have even prosecuted him at all, chalking it all up to defense of your household? I will never know. I still think about that. My client had since moved out of the state to get a new life away from the publicity and his infamous past. As a postscript, no one came to the county to claim the body of the victim.

I could not, for the life of me, figure out why the Deputy DA said what he said to the judge. I still cannot. The practice of law in a heavy-duty case with a great deal of publicity can be very stressful. I get that. I experience the same stress. Your client's life hangs on your words in court. But why would you jeopardize your own case. Sometimes personality conflicts between judges and lawyers can be critical. Try to avoid such conflicts. It could hurt you down the line.

17
Legal Secretary vs Law Firm

This matter did not occur in California or Wyoming, but in the state of Nevada, in a good- sized city. The Plaintiff was an employee of mine in the past, working as a legal secretary. She was a very nice-looking women, most would say she was a beautiful women. She was tall, shapely with blond hair and a wonderful personality. She was the kind of girl you would see in Vogue or Cosmopolitan magazines. She had moved over the Sierra Mountains to a city in Nevada, and, sought employment as a legal secretary in a large law firm.

The facts in the Nevada court file are as follows. At the law firm, the lawyers would play tricks on her repeatedly such as dropping pencils and asking her to pick them up, so they could view her derriere in a unique position, making remarks to her about her social life, asking her to do certain things that would accentuate various parts of her anatomy, propositioning her, etc. This went on for months. She finally left her employment and came to see me about this problem. My client was terribly upset over this, she had been constantly harassed, embarrassed, and eventually had to leave her employment, which resulted in a loss of income.

I am not licensed in Nevada, but I knew lawyers in the city where she was employed with which I had contact. I petitioned the Nevada Court to be admitted pro hac vice for this case alone. With the Nevada lawyer friend of mine, we sued the law firm for sexual harassment, intentional infliction of emotional distress, etc. We prepared the complaint, and as was usual in these cases the facts alleged in the complaint were quite descriptive.

Once the case was filed it made quite a stir within the community. The case and the law firm involved became the laughingstock of the city. Without my knowledge, the court clerks made copies of the complaint and began distributing the complaint with all the descriptive details to other firms, lawyers, and others. It was quite a carnival atmosphere.

I scheduled several depositions of the various witnesses and employees within the firm. These depositions would be all important and my opportunity to personally meet the lawyer defendants and assess their attitudes, credibility, and especially their willingness to permit this very humiliating action to continue in their own law firm. I asked another law firm if we could use their facilities for these depositions. They were more than happy to accommodate us.

The day for depositions arrived. We all gathered in a large room with me, and co-counsel, several defendant lawyers, defense counsel, and the court reporter. To say that you could cut the atmosphere with a knife was an understatement. Off the record, before the deposition began, several lawyers verbally jumped on me with a "who do you think you are suing us," and "where do you get the nerve to file such a disreputable complaint?" That went on and on. What they were saying was that lawyers do not eat their own. That professionalism should be to dismiss what had occurred within that firm as simply stress release, good natured fun, or whatever. I sat there and took their comments and snide remarks in stride. I let them sound off. It only illustrated the correctness of my position. But - only to a point. I asked the court reporter if she was ready and if she would swear in the witness.

At that point, the defense attorney asked to speak to me alone. We spoke for quite some time. He did not want this case to be tried nor did he wish the case to be prolonged any more than it had to. He wished it to be settled, and quickly. I knew this was going to happen for several reasons. First, the plaintiff was not only a fine- looking women, but it could readily be seen that if anyone would be sexually harassed it would be her. My client was also very sincere and credible. Every time she spoke of this she cried! Lawyers just love clients who cry.

Second, we did our homework and found that other women, within that firm, who quit their jobs were also sexually harassed. We even found a witness who was still employed and was willing to testify. Third, every lawyer knows sexual harassment is a viable cause of action and these lawyers knew better. We also knew that since these lawyers knew better, had superior knowledge, a jury would be more than happy to slap them down. In general, Lawyers are just not popular people. Fourth, we knew that the firm had suffered great damage by their inappropriate pastime and, as such, would be more than willing to settle lickety split.

Lawyers must calculate the hard, cold realities of all their cases. Some would say we are a cold bunch of bottom feeders, who are only interested in money and playing the system. If that were true, I would be a rich man. Lawyers have a job to do and must, for the benefit of their client, do whatever is necessary to gain as much advantage as they can or be eaten alive by an opposing attorney. A lawyer must constantly recalculate and reassess each case as the facts unfold. The system that has developed over these many centuries demands it. Speaking and representing issues for others is an awesome responsibility. There is nothing worse than making a critical error in fact, law, or judgment, and receiving that dreaded letter marked "confidential" from your State Bar.

After negotiating for several weeks, we did come to a settlement agreement. My client was compensated for her lost wages, embarrassment, humiliation, and possible punitive damages as punishment. It all involved a six-figure settlement, which I believed was very fair for all involved. I know the law firm knew that if it went to trial, they may have been hit for far more in damages. They had to make the same calculation. My client felt the settlement was fair. Just another happy customer.

18

Laughter Is the Best Medicine

My relationship with the courthouse Deputy Sheriffs was unique, to say the least. When you appeared in court as much as I did and saw the same guys every day, all week, every month, every year, you became friends. Some of these guys were hilarious as described in Chapter Ten. That one Bailiff just loved to play tricks on me. Once, at a sentencing hearing, he drew a picture of a gallows with a man hanging and had another bailiff hand it to me. Of course, my client was placed on probation, as I usually succeeded in my cases. After the hearing that bailiff would always say "good job."

Some deputies went out of their way to play practical jokes. In one instance, a pair of deputies placed a cardboard sign on the back of my SUV. I did not see the sign and drove around town back to my office. I did not notice the sign until I got back in the car and saw this white cardboard sign which said: "Will Sue for Food." I cannot imagine what the townsfolk thought as they saw that sign.

In another incident, the deputies prepared a document on official court stationery which gave probationer's a list of private facilities that offered community service hourly credits. In the documents they listed my name, phone number, office address as a facility they could work off their community credit hours. I'll be damned if the phone didn't start ringing and my secretary telling me that this or that man called asking to work off their hours at my office! I went to the courthouse to see what was going on. They showed me the probationer's community service list document. Sure enough, my name was listed. I did ask the head clerk about the document, and to please amend the list. She laughed and said she had an idea how my name got there. I laughed as well.

These deputies were relentless. I once found my briefcase handcuffed to a stair well; deputies would bring me coffee during a hearing, but with eight teaspoons of sugar, knowing I take mine black, no sugar. They found my car keys and attached 12 keys from lost and found to the key ring, etc. These fellows made the practice of law endurable. With all the stressful high-pressure cases I had going on, they made me not only survive the daily grind, but made me and others laugh. And laughter was the best medicine for a grunt in the trenches lawyer.

Sometimes, the laughter comes not from others, but from yourself. In one instance, I was grooming my horse, and placed my hand down on the ground while cutting the horse's fetlocks. Big mistake. The horse moved and stepped on my left hand with all his weight and broke my middle finger. I rather quickly put the horse away and went to the emergency room at our local hospital. The doctor examined the finger, and sure enough, it was broken. He had to set the finger. What he did was put that middle finger in a splint in such a way that I had a semi-permanent obscene gesture any time I would expose my left hand. I cannot say that the doctor set that finger in such a way to purposely make me a laughing-stock, but I have suspicions. Several days later, I was in court and during the hearing I kept my left arm inside my coat pocket. The judge could not help but notice and asked me to please remove my hand out of the coat. I explained to him the situation. He was not deterred. "It is ok, counsel, you look terribly uncomfortable with your hand in your jacket. Please remove your hand. So, I did. The judge was presented with the bird. That is, a full on flip off. Everyone was laughing. The judge, in his stoic manner, said, "counsel you may place your hand back in your coat jacket." To be sure, I have never, under any circumstances, ever flipped anyone off, for any reason in my entire life. As a footnote, my wife does that on a near daily basis! Why just the other day…Never mind.

19

Star Struck vs The Stage Diver

This was a different kind of personal injury matter and nothing like I had ever seen before in my practice, although the facts were familiar. It involved an enthusiastic spectator who was injured by the lead singer of a popular rock band at a concert in a huge arena in Sacramento. Having been in the entertainment business I was happy to have received this case. The only other case I knew of where there were unhappy spectators was the one, I witnessed while my band performed alongside Jeff Beck and Faces with Rod Stewart, back in the late sixties. In that matter, one of the band mates of Faces, not Rod Stewart, decided to spray the audience with a fire extinguisher. It did not end well. Sometimes your past blends in perfectly with your role as an attorney litigator.

The facts of this case as alleged by the civil complaint were as follows: a popular band was performing at Arco Arena in Sacramento on a given evening. This band was a popular attraction, and the Arena was full. My client was standing at the front of the stage apparently enjoying the music and the crowd's enthusiasm. He turned his back from the stage for a moment to speak to another person when the lead singer launched himself from the stage onto the crowd. I have learned that this is called "stage diving," something that was not done back when I was performing. The singer landed on my client's head causing serious head injuries, including a neck compression, concussion, injuring his vertebrae, etc.

He came to see me within several weeks of the incident and was still suffering from symptoms of the injuries, even after hospitalization. After due diligence of the facts of the case we filed suit against the band, the Arena, etc. The Defendants alleged that, yes, the concert took place, yes, the band performed, yes, the lead singer did "stage dive," as he sometimes, but not always, does in their performance, but that the plaintiff was not at that concert, and that the case must be dismissed.

I asked my client if we had witnesses as to his having been there. He went alone, we had no witnesses. Ok. Let's think. I know that sometimes there are video tapes used by arenas to record the events. We served on Defendants a Discovery Request for any and all video tapes that were being utilized at the night of the performance. Sure enough, we found that the Arena has multiple video tapes of the goings on during the concert, including the stage. We demanded video tapes. Defendant's counsel complied. Upon viewing the tapes, we could clearly see the Plaintiff at the front of the stage, clapping away at the music, then turning around to speak to a person, whereupon the lead singer takes a flying leap at the audience and lands directly on my client's head! At this point, Defendants motioned the court for a mediation to try and settle the matter rather than risk a trial. Bad public relations. The tape was all too definitive on the issue as to liability. I mean, there he was, minding his own business at a rock concert, when a 150-pound man lands on his head! My experience taught me that rock concerts can be dangerous to your health.

A mediation was set up at a neutral location. This is where the case gets interesting. Some of the band mates appear at the mediation. My client is stunned if not enamored over their appearance at the mediation. He was bug eyed. The usual give and take goes on, the arguing your position and the damages from both sides. The two parties separate into two rooms and speak to the mediator one side at a time in an effort to hammer out each side's position. Defendants come back with an offer. I say "no," the amount is insufficient. My client says, "I want free tickets to their next concert." The mediator and I look at each other with a puzzled look. The mediator leaves to see the Defendants. They come back with a higher offer. I say "no," not enough, "we want this....", and give various reasons for our position. The client again says: "we also want free tickets to the next concert." The mediator and I again look at each other, wondering where my client is coming from. I ask to speak to my client alone.

The mediator leaves us alone to discuss this issue and he goes to speak to the Defendants. We discuss this demand by the Plaintiff. My client tells me that no matter what settlement is reached he wants free tickets to their next concert. I tell him that this is not the time, nor the place for this demand. "You have been injured by their actions," I said. Since you have suffered serious injuries, asking for tickets shows weakness and a display that you're not taking this seriously. However, he insisted that he wanted those tickets. I told him not to mention any tickets anymore, since I believed it was not in the client's interests to bring this up. He reluctantly agrees.

The Defendants finally make an acceptable offer that fairly compensates the Plaintiff for his injuries, including medical bills, pain, suffering and residual damages. All parties get together again to hammer out on paper the settlement made and accepted. Toward the end, my client states, "but I also want free tickets to their next concert." Dead silence. The band mates chime in and say: "sure let's give him free tickets." My client is happy, incredibly happy. He makes peace with the band mates and gets his free tickets. He also gets fairly compensated. I became the hero.

20

MOVING ON

After 23 years of energetic practice, I began to feel the symptoms of burnout. We lawyers know what burn out feels like. You start losing your patience with clients. You find yourself engaging in yelling matches with opposing attorneys. Your disagreements with judges become more pronounced. All aspects of your life suffer. Your relationship with those you love suffers, and prescription Prozac becomes a fact of life. It is at those times that you must reconstruct your lifestyle. To stem the tide of burn out, my wife and I would take road trips to Wyoming, bring our horses, and play cowboy on various ranches we were familiar with. On these numerous trips we made quite a few friends in Wyoming. We felt relaxed by being out in the wilderness, herding cows, hanging out with real cowboys and Indians, listening to their amazement at a Brooklynite and Lawyer wanting their way of life, working on real cattle ranches.

The only problem we had was that after a couple of weeks we had to go home and deal with the many problems our clients suffered from. There was one trip we made in late March, early April that was so pleasurable, we felt that perhaps we could relocate to Wyoming, purchase some land and semi-retire. Wow, what an idea! This is a hard decision to make. You spent years building a law practice. You have quite a bit of success in the clients you had and in their success in the various cases and matters. Most of all, it is difficult to give up the financial security you built up over the years.

Moving to a rural area is one thing. Moving to a place like Wyoming where the state population is smaller than the city of Sacramento can be quite a change. It is a place where the towns are smaller than a city block, where the cows outnumber people 3-1, where a traffic jam is a herd of antelope crossing the highway, and where you must travel 35 miles to the closest town that can support a Walmart. Why would I do this, you may ask? It was time for a change. It was time to see another side of life, a side we had never experienced before. Peace and solitude - what a thought! Most of all, I needed a break.

Of the many things about America that I love is there are so many opportunities, so many ways you can reinvent yourself, so many things you can do in which you can change your life - for the better. You must have the courage to do it, to not be afraid of change. Change can be good. So, we closed our law practice, packed up our furniture, belongings, horses, dogs, and cats and moved to Wyoming. We bought a 37-acre parcel of land, built a wonderful house and built a small horse ranch. It took us over a year to do this. We worked on the house and surroundings night and day. It was a labor of love.

Living in Wyoming is different, as I am sure Kanye West and Kim Kardashian have discovered. The people here are conservative, hard-working, religious, and have unshakable beliefs. The people here believe that people should pull their own weight. They do not tolerate the "victim" attitude well. Wyoming certainly is not California. The people here revel in their freedom. Unless you live within the confines of the large towns and small cities, building permits are unheard of. You build what you want, when you want it without an overbearing government looking over your shoulder. They build good, quality homes there, since to build a bad one is a death knell for their business. Every household is armed. It's a way of life here. Open carry is common and concealed carry is also common since the state legislature permitted concealed carry without a permit. Funny thing is that Wyoming has never had a mass shooting and is one of the safest states in this union. Go figure.

However, they can be suspicious of newcomers. They do not wish to change their lifestyle and resent those that try. They resent and are concerned with those that come here and make judgment calls on the Wyoming attitudes toward public land use, wolves, grizzlies, etc. I was in lock step with the residents' attitude and my belief was only reinforced when I represented one of those ranchers that lost 35 plus calves to a pack of wolves. I have seen wolves attack a buffalo calf and tear it to shreds. Not a pretty sight. I have seen herds of hundreds of elk disappear because of wolf predation. You don't see large herds of elk anymore in wolf country. I could say more but I'll save it. Many times, I have seen bumper stickers that say: "This ain't California, go home."

It took a while to be accepted. After all, I had two strikes against me from the start. I was a lawyer and came from California. They will keep their distance until they know you. It took a while, but we blended in perfectly. We volunteered to help at ranches, brandings, gatherings, rounding up cows, etc. It was fun, not work for us. The people here have a good time attitude and sense of humor. After all, the work is hard, the country is rough, and the winters are even rougher.

I will tell you a story about being a newcomer here. We had hired a farrier to take care of our horses' feet, trim, shoe, whatever they needed. This man, late 50's, was an all- around good guy. He was friendly, outspoken, and a good talker. While shoeing horses he stated: "The wife and I have been talkin about you two." "Oh?" I said, "Yeah. We've all been wonderin what you all are doin out here." "You live far from town, have this big house, with two floors where you can see all around. You have Doberman dogs, and I have seen all the guns you have on your walls — and your name is DiLorenzo. That's an 'I' talian name, isn't it? And you're a lawyer to boot, from California, no less. We all think you are in the Federal Witness Protection Program, aren't you?" The only response I could think of was: "shhhhh."

In time, we became so community and politically active that we befriended many movers and shakers, and our home became a center of activities that included picnics and lectures in which hundreds of people attended including three United States senators, two Congressman, a Vice President, nationally known personalities, a rock star, media and news people from as far away as The London Daily Telegraph. It was a lot of fun.

We stayed out of the law for only about a year. Rural lawyers are one thing in the California countryside. But in Wyoming, it's a whole different ball game. It is a small legal community, even closer and more intimate than rural California. I quickly made friends, and with many of them. I have always been into the social whirl, and Wyoming was no exception. Every Christmas we have a big dinner at the house for all the District Court clerks. Such good friends. The real power in the courts.

I have been a lawyer in California for nearly 24 years. I knew my stuff. But I needed to gain admission to the Bar in Wyoming. Not easy. California is one of those states that will not admit any out of state lawyers unless they take the Bar exam. No reciprocity. None. What that means is without reciprocity, Wyoming will not give reciprocity. Which tells you that you must again endure the taking of a Bar exam. The one event most lawyers fear most. However, you do what you must do and take the damn Bar exam.

As a new Wyoming lawyer, being a California lawyer in Wyoming has its ups and downs. You will be tormented, albeit in good fun. As an example, I was at a motion hearing in a neighboring county. I presented my argument at length to the District Court Judge. At the conclusion of my argument, the Judge looked at me for a moment, then said, "Is this one of those California lawyers' tricks?" The court laughed. I was a bit stunned and did not know what to say. The Judge smiled and said: "lighten up counsel."

In another incident, I was scheduled for a pre-trial conference on a felony matter. In this county all felony matters are calendared for the same day for conferences to determine their status as to whether there will be a disposition or a trial. We all waited in the judges' chambers waiting room. The room was full. Several public defenders were there, private attorneys, and a couple of deputy County counsels were present. While waiting I placed my hat, a fine Stetson, and my pride and joy, on the credenza. I left for a moment to the Circuit Court to file paperwork. When I came back to a still filled noisy room, I noticed that my hat contained a microphone and a paper party hat. I sat down on the sofa with my hat in my lap wondering what the hell a microphone and party hat was doing in my beloved Stetson. I picked up the microphone and party hat, and at that precise moment, two district Court Judges burst into the room, wherein one of them shouted at me: "Mr. DiLorenzo, how many times do I have to tell you that these chambers are not a Karaoke Bar!" Every lawyer burst out laughing at the fact that I was caught unaware, unprepared, and with nothing to say, which was a rarity! I will never forget that!

21
The Wild West Still Lives

I have always loved the "Old West." There is something terribly romantic and mysterious about the wide-open plains and mountains. The lack of people, buildings, roads, and the open sky for as far as you can see is remarkable to gaze at. The wildlife is all still there. I have packed in on horseback numerous times and have seen wolves, grizzlies, moose, herds of buffalo and elk in magnificent places. Many think this is all gone, that what our forefathers saw and experienced can no longer be seen or felt. You could not be more wrong. Much of it is all still there in so many corners of these United States. You just must look for it.

Wyoming has a colorful history, to say the least. This is a place in which Big Nose George killed two lawmen and bragged about it in 1880, long enough to be caught and hanged by a mob of vigilantes in 1881. A citizen skinned him and had a pair of shoes made from Big Nose George. That didn't seem terribly unusual since that citizen wore those shoes at his inauguration when they elected him Governor of the State of Wyoming in 1893! Wyoming is...different.

On my many trips to Wyoming I met a ranching family that I became quite friendly with. This family had been ranching on their "spread" of many thousands of acres for many years, since 1891. The ranch was beautiful. The land was and is a picture postcard, with tall grass, majestic mountain ranges in the background and, I must say, quite isolated. Rough country. But the people who inhabit these places are just as rough.

I had known members of that family from my past experiences on their ranch. There were four siblings that were raised on that isolated ranch that spanned two states. These people were not gentle souls. They were used to a hard life and certainly looked the part. In my life in South Brooklyn, I had known tough people. Some of the families my parents knew back in the day were not gentle souls. But no one I knew back then could compare with these folks. They were used to cold winters to the tune of below zero, of calving in the pitch darkness in the middle of nowhere, in the wee hours of the morning that would make you shrink from even the thought of it. I truly admire these people. They are the stuff that built this nation of ours.

The two girls had hands as tough as sandpaper and would use felt pens as eyeliner. One of the boys had one arm, the other shot off when a teenager. The other was more sedate, but tall, thin, and quite competent. They were all surprisingly well read and world-wise. In the late hours in winter, when they had no TV, there was nothing to do but read. They knew what was going on. Their mom, half white, half native American was just as tough. That woman was hard.

My only criticism of the ranches and the cowboys who work them is that none of the ranch hands or their cooks knew how to make coffee. One would think these hands would demand strong coffee for what they are to endure in the day ahead. Certainly not the case. Their coffee is so weak and flavorless that it is undrinkable belly wash to anyone who knows anything about good coffee. One would think ground coffee was a rare and precious commodity, the stingy way in which they are distributed to the coffee pot. The quality of coffee does not change from ranch to ranch either. It's as if they all got together and compared notes.

On one of my trips to their ranch, by a campfire at their cow camp, they started to tell me of a problem with a neighbor. The neighbor was in fact the new husband of a cousin of theirs. This cousin, through her family, owned a great deal of land contiguous to their ranch. At an obscure corner of both land holdings there was a small pass in which herds of cows passed in spring and fall roundups. That pass was vital to the ranch and was the only convenient way in which they could herd the cows from one pasture to the next. That pass was used by that family for many decades in the past. The problem was that the small pass was on land owned by their cousin.

It seemed that for whatever reason I could not figure out why the husband of that cousin refused to permit the neighboring ranchers to use that pass, and I mean refused big time. They told me that he would dress up in camo with an AR-15 and gate off the pass making it impossible for the cows to pass through. Wow, this was a problem. I did not think this would be a big legal problem since it seemed clear to me that the family had a prescriptive easement through that pass and held it for decades. The real problem was that this guy who was always armed to the teeth whenever any ranching cowboys were in the area and refused to permit them to traverse through the pass. I had no idea what this family had done to him in the past to make him so belligerent. I asked if you could simply talk to your cousin about the problem. That sounded like the easiest solution. She was their first cousin, and she and her parents had always permitted them to use that pass. I was told that they had tried. The land belonged to her. But apparently, she was no longer in control of the situation and wanted no part in her husband's dispute with that family. Something did not seem right with all of this. But they asked me to intervene to help solve the problem.

They wanted me to see the issue first-hand and took me to that pass. Sure, why not. We hopped into an old four-wheel drive pickup and traveled to their main "home ranch" first to pick up some items. The house was nothing to look at. It was old, very worn, and looked as if it was slapped together. A distance from the house I was shown a small graveyard of family members that had been buried there for a hundred years. One would think you would not see such things anymore, but you would be wrong. While I was there, that old mom showed me where she was to be buried, when the time came.

They invited me in. It was a scene I will never forget. The interior was just as unimpressive as the exterior. It too looked like it was slapped together. It was large on the inside since I could not see any bedrooms. It was just one big room, a wood stove for heat, and a makeshift bathroom that was decades out of date. I dare not go in there. They had antique firearms all over the walls dating back over a century of arms used by their long dead family members. "This is my great grandfather's rifle, my other grandfathers Colt revolver." I have seen less collections in firearms museums. On the floors were items found on the ranch over many years such as numerous buffalo skulls, huge bones from what I could not even guess at. The "Knickknacks" on the floors and the walls were worth far more than the house that contained it all.

What was remarkable to me was that their thousands of acres of deeded and leased land were worth a fortune in dollars, yet they lived a marginal existence. Their lifestyle, which consisted of being land wealthy and cash poor was common amongst many out there. They were not the only ones. Millions of dollars of land and living like this? I can tell you in all honesty, I believe few could live that lifestyle unless you were born to it. I have an enormous amount of respect for those people.

Now I understand why these ranchers believe what they believe. These are the descendants of the pioneers, the ones who settled this land and lived side by side with and intermarried amongst the native populations, and as they tell it, lived in peace with them all. They will live and die on that land. The only enemy they have, as they tell it, is the intrusive government which continually tries to make it as difficult for them as possible. They find the wolf reintroduction as just another example of government interference in their way of life. When you live a marginal existence, every calf is valuable at the sale stock yard. A loss to wolves means less money for groceries for the family. Every rancher out there that I met will tell of many lost calves to these predators, and thus lost income, and parts to repair their old trucks. For them it is survival. You will see bumper stickers that say "Welcome to Wyoming. Now take a wolf and go home." They just want to be left alone.

When all was ready at the home ranch, we took that long trip through open country to that pass. What a place. The country was magnificent, the creeks were flowing, the grass was high, the sky was huge. When we arrived what I saw was a small pass-through large rock, boulders and a forest that was not over twenty feet wide. You could see the beaten down track of many years of cows and wildlife running through from one end to the other to get to that next pasture to feed and water.

Sure enough, while gazing at this sight I saw a man, in his late thirties, in full camo gear watching us intently. He was carrying a rifle (it wasn't hunting season). This guy was strange, both in his behavior and his appearance. What disturbed me the most was the smile he had on his face; a bizarre, almost nefarious smile that said please cross the line so I can shoot your ass off. This man wanted trouble. Was asking for it. You could see it all over him. Coming from South Brooklyn, I don't scare much. But he scared me plenty. It was that grin. Whenever we moved to view the pass, he moved with us, clutching that rifle. Yes, that was their cousin's husband.

After this rather worrisome visit to the scene of the issue, we set up a meeting between their family lawyer in Montana and me to figure out a solution to the problem. Several days later, while meeting with some members of the family and their lawyer at his office, a secretary came in the room to tell us that their dear cousin by marriage was just found dead, that morning. We all looked at each other. Their Montana lawyer panicked and told them, especially the two brothers who were there, not to say anything to anybody about any of this. The lawyer was doing exactly what a good lawyer is supposed to do. Perhaps he knew something I didn't, or he knew the propensity of certain members of that family? I do not know. But, by all accounts, the death was of natural causes. That family, through the coincidental misfortune of another, had their problem solved.

Suddenly, the entire easement problem, with all its related difficulties disappeared. The problem that had plagued that family was gone. Just gone. They could now use that pass as they had done since the nineteenth century.

22

The Russian Connection

This case was awful and can show how far down the road to perdition a lawyer can go to harm their own client, their own career and eventually their own lives for pure self-interest and profit. My client was a Russian immigrant to the United States when he was only a small child. He was adopted by wealthy people from New Jersey who tragically died in an airplane crash back east when my client was a teenager. He inherited a great deal of money from his adoptive parents' estate of which all was placed in a trust. The monies placed in that trust were in the millions.

A trustee to handle the management of the trust was named. The trust was being administered by a Wyoming attorney. Soon after this attorney began to be involved in the trust, she started buying properties and taking trips to Europe. It should be mentioned that the trustor was not a sophisticated individual when it came to handling money or even paying bills. English was still his second language. My client was married at the time and had three children. The wife wore the pants in that family. He simply did what was told to him. His administrator took full advantage of my client's lack of understanding except that the wife became suspicious.

On one occasion, the administrator wired $100,000 to her personal account. On another occasion she wired $20,000 to herself, and only transferred $10,000 to the trustor. On another occasion, she wired $35,000 to herself and only $10,000 to the trustor. On yet another occasion she transferred $250,000 to herself, and again, another $225,000 to her personal account. She kept transferring sums to herself, all in all, the sum of $704,000 was wrongfully transferred to her personal account!

I was retained when it became obvious that a great deal of money was missing that did not flow to the young trustor. We prepared a suit against the attorney administrator and the FBI became involved since the attorney was involved in wire fraud. We must have spent days with the FBI trying to figure out all the monies that were taken when it was taken and to whom it was sent. It was determined that the attorney indeed had embezzled on or about $704,000 from the trust.

This was a serious matter. The attorney trust administrator could not only lose her license to practice but she was facing many years in a federal prison. She retained an attorney from out of town. Her attorney was a man I knew quite well. He was about my age, practiced law as long as I have, well respected and knew his stuff. He wanted a meeting to discuss the problem. I am always willing to talk to any attorney about any case. We met and it was acknowledged that his client had indeed committed this offense and wanted to rectify the matter. After several long discussions over several weeks, we had made a tentative agreement.

The monies were to be returned in the sum of $750,000 in cash and real properties. All in all, the sum to be settled was perfectly secured with both the cash transferred and the real properties that were to be appraised to equal the sum of the settlement figure.   There was nothing I could do in so far as the FBI and their investigation.   All I could do was perhaps tell the court that the Defendant has been compensated and reimbursed for the loss.   That was acceptable to opposing counsel.

I called my client to have a meeting with him as to the confirmed settlement offer. I explained in detail what the offer included. The offer was the sum of $750,000 in full and fair compensation for my client's loss.   The offer included $350,000 in cash, plus Defendant would deed three of her rental properties to the Plaintiff. Each property would be appraised by a real estate appraiser as to the fair market value to make sure the values met the expected value of the settlement offer. The properties were owned free and clear of any mortgages, so it would be an easy transfer. I had a complete list of all her properties and was shown her tax records to help confirm her assets.

My client seemed pleased. But not everyone was happy. My client's wife and father-in-law were incensed by the offer. They started yelling at me.   I could not believe their attitude. The wife wanted a million dollars with a threat to have the lawyer put in jail. I informed them that I could not do that and could not use a threat of criminal action in a civil case. I specifically told them that the FBI was handling that matter and could not interfere.   I tried to explain the Rules of Professional Responsibility that prevented me from taking such action. They were not listening. They were far too angry with me to even consider the offer.   I explained to them that if this matter went to trial, they may not get as much as they are now demanding. Not only that, I explained, once you get a judgment you must try and collect it, and that could be the biggest problem.   A trial would place the Defendant in the position of spending all her money on lawyers rather than compensating the Plaintiff.

No dice. I was fired by the wife and the father-in-law. Not the client, but the wife and the father-in-law demanded my withdrawal. My client was Russian born. English was a second language. The real problem here was his wife, a walking bipolar disorder, who was impossible to get along with. He did not have the chutzpah to challenge his wife or father-in-law on their demand to fire me. I really felt sorry for this guy. I believed they were leading him astray, to a potential disaster.

I withdrew from the case. They hired another lawyer who took the matter to trial. This young lawyer was confident, too confident. The parties spent many months in litigation, discovery, motions all of which resulted in a week-long trial. Many months means many dollars spent on lawyers that could have been used to compensate the Plaintiff. The trial court decided in my former client's favor but awarded only $ 650,000, $100,000 less than the offer I received. My former client did not recoup his loss, collected only about $300,000. The attorney-trustee exhausted much of her liquid assets, sold some properties, to pay her attorney fees. She even gifted some properties to family members. She then committed suicide with a drug overdose. A sad ending.

The lesson to be learned here is that a good lawyer knows what they can squeeze from any given defendant, and what they cannot. When they do their homework, they know what can be done and what cannot be accomplished. They also know that a trial always has its risks. That no matter what you think you can prove, there is always the risk that you will be snookered. The offer I worked hard to put on paper was a good one and the most that could be made given the assets that we had to work with.

There is another lesson to be learned. Always listen to an old lawyer with years of experience. They know the system. They can predict nearly every outcome in every fact pattern. Ignore them to your peril.

As an aside, this was yet another case in which the FBI was involved. They asked me for my files. My client insisted I give it to them and share information. Hundreds of thousands of dollars were stolen by the lawyer and wired to her account. After months of working on the case, the FBI lost interest and dropped the matter! Why, I cannot fathom. It seemed to me they were very interested in "preserving the integrity of the banking system" as in chapter 6. But when it comes to protecting the little guy, well, they don't have the time. They would rather have 20 armed agents serve an arrest warrant on a small town right-to-life pastor, with six kids. Pitiful.

23
A Head Case

This case involved a husband and wife. The couple always seemed to be happy. We knew them from our social contacts. They are both hard working people. These were good people. Salt of the earth types. It is always heartbreaking to be legally involved with people of this quality, to be in trouble. Your emotions get involved and can affect your thinking and objectivity. You must remain objective and cool, and handle it like any other case, or else you do your client no good at all. It is always risky to take cases from acquaintances, friends, and family. They expect more from you than strangers.

The facts, as stated in the court files, are these: the couple were watching TV but could not get the satellite to work properly. They had just finished dinner and had a few beers. Alcohol and arguments always seem to go together. It is not clear what started the argument, but it seems it had something to do with their TV reception and the lack of signals. This TV problem apparently escalated into an argument. The argument turned into a violent confrontation in which the husband started to hit his wife with his drum set drum pedal. He was arrested and charged with felony aggravated assault.

I got a call from the victim, his wife. Having the wife call-in to seek a lawyer in this type of case is rather common. Even the best of marriages experiences some problems. Sometimes when there is stress due to money, children, work, arguments happen. I have seen it many times in my forty years.

One of the officers that responded to the call was a deputy I knew. We had known each other for years. We had cowboyed together on a friend's ranch before he was a deputy. This is what happens when you practice law in a very small rural community. Everybody knows everybody. The courts in Wyoming know this and give you leeway.

But you must do your job. Your client is the most important person in the world. Any relationships you have with any witnesses or law enforcement must be set aside and dealt with. Since the matter never went to trial or a hearing on a motion to suppress evidence, the relationship issue became moot.

In any case, the victim's husband was in jail. The wife wanted to talk to me and told me he had not been himself lately. She was genuinely concerned about her husband's health. She wanted me to go see him in the county jail. This did not sound good. I had known this man for years, and he always seemed to be a gentle soul. I was very curious as to how this could have happened. I wanted to see him as quickly as I could get there. My gut feeling told me I needed my investigator friend to go with me. He was a retired Master Sergeant in the USMC, and a retired police officer. He knew his stuff. I knew he would be able to help.

On the way to the jail, I picked up my retired police officer investigator and asked him to notice anything that seemed out of the ordinary. When we saw my client in jail, he began to cry. Breaks your heart. We had a long talk as to what had happened. He told me everything. My investigator gave him an eye test, a test he gave people who were suspected of drunk and intoxicated driving. We continued to talk and told my client that things would get better, that I would set the matter for a bail hearing and get him out of jail.

On the way home, my investigator friend told me he has nystagmus, that his eyes were not moving properly. Time had passed, so my client was perfectly sober, so, how could he suffer from nystagmus? Nystagmus occurs when there is some form of brain misfunction or that something in the brain that regulates the eye movement and positioning does not work properly. I decided that my client needed to be released as soon as I can get into court, and that a full medical exam on my client needed to be done as quickly as possible. I wanted to know whether there was a brain malfunction somewhere else that affected other than eye movement. I got him released on bond and we sent him to a hospital for a full medical exam, including an MRI brain scan. Knowing my client was a farrier, I asked him questions as to whether he had ever been kicked in the head. He said yes, a few years ago. He also told me that he fell off a ladder and hit his head some time ago. The bond conditions included stay away orders, but with permission to travel to see doctors in Montana. We pled Not guilty by Reason of Mental Illness. I received the police reports and the photos of the victim's wife. The photos were not pretty, on the contrary. And the police reports were to the point and seemed open and shut.

In Wyoming, any such plea automatically requires an examination by the Wyoming Department of Health in accordance with the Wyoming statutes. An order for such an evaluation was filed by the court. This was done to assist the court in the determination of my client's mental state at the time of the incident. It was determined by the Health Department that my client had multiple head injuries including multiple concussions playing football, kicked in the head by a horse at age twelve, in addition to his recent head injury from a horse two days prior to the incident, plus falling off a ladder. Radiological consultations revealed the tumor or lesions in the frontal lobe region of his brain, and white matter lesions as well. The client's doctor and psychiatrist were of the opinion that these numerous concussive injuries could have resulted in structural damage to the brain, potentially impacting the client's personality and judgment. However, no doctor I employed could definitively state that such damage could wholly account for any specific behavioral incident.

However, the Wyoming Department of health believed my client did understand the wrongfulness of his actions. But because of his neurological dysfunction he was incapable of managing his behavior appropriately. This was a classic "irresistible impulse" situation, of which, the State of Wyoming does not recognize. Wyoming is not California.

Yes, my client suffered from a tumor in his frontal lobe, and the tumor was growing. The tumor was affecting his judgment and impulse control. My clients' anger was more difficult to keep in check. This case raised complex and troubling questions about how the courts define criminal behavior and responsibility. This defense is troublesome, however, since even the most sophisticated brain scans cannot seem to show a direct correlation between a specific crime and brain dysfunction. I do believe, however, that my client's tumor did, indeed, contribute to his inability to control his anger. However, we could not establish that it was the direct cause of his actions. Although criminal lawyers have been increasingly raising such questions in criminal defense cases, this would be a rather novel defense here in Wyoming.

What do we do now? I did not believe I could successfully use the tumor as a complete defense against the crime charged. A trial and conviction would not help my client. I was not going to gamble on my client's future. If I take the matter

114

to trial, he would most probably be convicted and sent to prison. The County Attorney's attitude was that the defendant had beaten his wife with a deadly instrumentality with such force as to convince a jury of his guilt. They had the photos to prove it. I told them that the wife would not testify. They said the wife already made far too many incriminating statements to the police on the day it happened. The County Attorney stated they would subpoena the wife to testify, that even if she did not show up, they could convict without her testimony. This was problematic since the wife did not want this incident to happen again, yet she did not want to testify against her husband and wanted to keep the marriage. I could not be sure how all this was going to go down. Even if she did testify for her husband, the statements she made to the police would sink my client. You can never be sure in these cases. Anything can happen. To my mind, and in my experience, you can never completely depend on the testimony of any spouse in this type of case. The situation with the marriage may have been somewhat chaotic and in such a case, I could not reasonably rely on anything said by the wife.

Since we had pled the defense of Not Guilty by Reason of Mental Illness, and since no doctor, even our own, could affirm the plea, after consultation with my client, we had to withdraw the plea. Under the circumstances, we pled guilty to the felony count but asked for a half day sentencing hearing. This is where you must pull a rabbit out of a hat.

The hearing was one of my dog and pony shows. I had doctors testify, psychiatrists, the victim, and so on. The prosecutor wanted six years, no probation. A harsh request to the Court. They argued for it. I argued against it, stating that justice had a more fitting determination. I wanted probation and a suspended sentence. All my witnesses argued that the defendant may not have been in control of his actions, lack of impulse control, or irresistible impulse. Not a defense, but I argued it was a mitigating factor that should be taken into consideration in sentencing.

After careful consideration, the Court at the hearing decided that the defendant was to serve a term of two years and not more than four years in state prison but that the term was suspended and that he was to be placed on 5 years' probation. Relief! No prison, no jail time. A big win. My client and his wife were joyful. I have seen both since. My client is under medical care on a regular basis. They have endured this tragic situation and have become better for it. I love it when that happens. A word about this judge. This presiding judge I have always known to be thoughtful and fair, one of the best judges I have known in this type of case. I knew that if I presented the facts, the medical testimony, the judge would not send this good man to prison. This judge, like so many I have seen, is very reluctant to send anyone to prison and will always look to an alternative, if the defense attorney is smart enough to give him one. I was right. This case shows where California judges and Wyoming judges display little difference in the manner in which they dispose of cases. In California, the judges would have done the same. And did, as in the Nam Vet cases in Chapters 11 and 16.

Several years later I saw my old client on the street. We stopped and talked. He looked well and he said he and his wife were doing well. The tumor was still growing but he was being medically treated for it and it seemed to be working. A success story.

24
The Barking at The Moon Case

This case came to me from a friend. This little old lady was given a citation for a barking dog nuisance. The charge was made by a neighbor who lived in the rear of her residence. It seems that when her little dog went to the back yard she would yap at the neighbor. This all took place within an incorporated small city in Wyoming. Then again, all cities in Wyoming are small.

At first, my reaction to the case was, "what! My career has now been reduced to a dog barking case!" Sometimes, you need to put aside your ego and do the right thing. That's what grunt lawyers do. I took this case because I liked this lady very much. She was about 85 years old, truly kind, community oriented. She often would have social functions at her home and in her backyard. She was a nice lady who went to church every Sunday, was quite politically active, and, over the years, seems to have had disagreements with her neighbor. The neighbor, on the other hand, was somewhat disagreeable and prickly. Every time that little dog went to the back yard, that neighbor would scold the little dog, or make gestures at the little guy and the old lady. How much could you possibly charge for a dog barking case?

I decided, as always, to do some investigation of the facts. We went to see the other neighbors to see if that dog was a nuisance, as charged. Every neighbor we spoke to insisted that it was the neighbor who was a nuisance and not my client. However, my father, God rest his soul, always warned me that "you cannot fight city hall." I always remembered that. As true as that phrase is in Brooklyn, well, maybe this time you can.

I had several conferences with the City Attorney but to no avail. I could not convince this man to drop the citation. Ok, let's calendar the matter for trial. I spoke to the court clerk and told her that we need to schedule the trial. She asked if a half day is enough. I said, no, I need two to three days. Dead silence on the phone. "You need what?" I need two to three days, please. "I will tell the judge, "She said.

What I had done is I had prepared 12 subpoenas to be served on all the neighbors we had spoken to. I filed the subpoenas with the court. I was going to march those witnesses in close order drill to that Court and have them testify as to the real nuisance in the neighborhood. Shortly afterward, I received an irate phone call from the City Attorney. "You subpoenaed 12 witnesses?!" "Yes, I did." I told him that each one of those witnesses will add a unique experience they have had with the complaining party, and that it is that party who is the nuisance. The City Attorney was even angrier than before. "We cannot waste three days on a dog barking case!" He said, "Well, it is what it is". He hung up the phone. Twenty minutes later he called back and told me he was going to dismiss the citation, and that he could not justify that expense on a barking dog. Look, this City Attorney is a good guy, trying to do the best he can under the circumstances. He must represent the city. I too, have a client to represent. And for some clients, no matter is too small.

118

My client, that little old lady, and her little dog, were as happy as could be. The moral to the story is that you can fight city hall. That is, if you can find a way to inconvenience them enough.

25
The Doctor Is Not In

This case was disturbing on many fronts. It involves my four "hates." First, I hate illicit drugs and what they do to good people. Second, I hate to see fine, educated people with everything to live for destroy themselves. Third, I hate it when these good people simply cannot accept the fact that they have a severe problem and refuse to accept that responsibility and take the cure. Last, I hate that habitual drug users destroy good families and ruin relationships.

This involved a defendant who was a licensed medical doctor who had a drug problem. The abuse of drugs belongs to every stratum of society, from the poor to the rich. It very much also belongs to the educated, and successful upper crust. Health care professionals are not immune to this national disaster. In fact, doctors and nurses account for one of the highest rates of addiction in the nation. According to USA Today, "Across the country, more than 100,000 doctors, nurses, technicians and other health professionals struggle with abuse or addiction, mostly involving narcotics such as Oxycodone and Fentanyl." (USA Today, Doctors, Medical

Staff on Drugs Put Patients at Risk, April 15, 2014, Peter Eisler).

I knew this doctor and retained him on occasion to consult with regarding various clients who had certain medical and emotional problems. He was good at what he did and had helped many people within this small rural cowboy community. He would even take on cases without a fee! In fact, this doctor was the lead witness for the defense in my own cases. He would complete a full exam of my clients and make recommendations to the court, which the court would always follow. The Court listened intently and accepted his opinions. Now, it was the good doctor who needed help, and lots of it.

The doctor was one of those 100,000 plus medical professionals who had a drug problem. He was in trouble previously with his medical license in another state but managed to duck that arrow. The doctor had a file with the medical professional authorities. He was also previously involved with another drug matter but managed to skate with that as well. But this time the charges were more serious.

Statements in the court file stated that the doctor had left his office in a somewhat inebriated manner. His secretary stated he was "not right." He hops into his vehicle and starts "huffing." For those of you who do not know what "huffing" is, I will explain. It is when an individual takes a pressurized can of, say, 'Dust Off,' places the air tip in his nostrils, presses the button and ingests the air which is a mixture of pressurized air and other vapors that will give you a mind-altering effect. 'Dust-Off' is readily available in most office supply stores and used to clean computers, and electronic gear. Canned air is essentially a toxic poison and can lead to psychological and physical addiction.

So, there is my client driving down the street allegedly huffing a can of 'Dust-Off.' He makes a turn, drives down a street and hits another vehicle in a head on collision. The driver of the second vehicle is a nice old lady and is seriously injured. The police are called to the scene, find my client in an intoxicated condition, inspect his vehicle, and see a can of 'Dust-Off' on the front seat of this vehicle. The doctor is arrested for felony intoxicated driving. After a review by the County Attorney, the man is charged with felony assault with a deadly instrumentality, his vehicle. This is a serious charge.

I was contacted first by the doctor for a consultation, then by his 80-year-old mother who asked that I take the case and that she would pay the retainer and all subsequent billings. Knowing the doctor and his past indiscretions with drugs I knew this would not be an easy case. After all, this time someone had been hurt! After putting my name on the case, I was contacted by the Medical Board as to his license to practice medicine. They had suspended his license on a temporary basis, at least until the criminal case was over. Under the circumstances, I suggested that he voluntarily suspend his license. This would prevent a hearing by the Medical Board and would give him a much better chance at regaining his license back when the criminal matter was over. As difficult as this was, he decided to take my advice.

My client was out on bail with the usual bond conditions, of no alcohol, drugs, and so on. Bail conditions are not exactly onerous. Just simply stay away publicly from alcohol and drugs. If you absolutely must have a drink, do it at home, at night, when you are not expected to go anywhere for anything. But no, I got a call that my client was arrested for being under the influence. He was riding his bicycle and crashed the bike on an inanimate object, fell, receiving bruises on his legs and arm. Of course, he was intoxicated and had a pint of whiskey in his back pocket. He was arrested for being under the influence of alcohol and for violations of bond conditions. As if things could not get even worse, then, they are. This man was a serious and hard-core alcohol and drug user.

We now have some difficult problems here. We have an underlying case in which he had been under the influence while driving and had caused serious injuries to an innocent lady. He then, it could be assumed by the court, still did not take the charges seriously since, it was alleged, he violated his bond conditions, was found intoxicated yet again, causing injury to himself. He also had a past DUI conviction. It does not get much worse, when you have a past conviction, then re-offend causing a serious injury, then re-offend again while out on bail. I was sure this man was going to spend some time in custody. The only question was the amount of time.

We worked hard on this one, but the facts are the facts. There is just so much you can do. My client very much needed that reality check. The good doctor has been in treatment three times in the past fifteen years. Still, we have a man who cannot control himself and his propensities for drugs and alcohol. And yet it seemed to me that he was still in denial. He would not go to in-patient treatment. I believed it was the only thing that could save him. But no dice. He refused to go. At least it would have shown to the court that he was sincere in taking the cure.

What made it infinitely worse, the victim in all of this was off work for six months and still had a lot of pain in her arm, back and neck. The victim's impact statement to the probation department was not pretty. After months of working on this matter, wheeling, and dealing, we had a situation in which if my client pled to the felony, he would be placed on five years' supervised probation with an opportunity of unsupervised probation after two years. We did receive a good pre-plea pre-sentence report in which they did not recommend any incarceration. The prosecuting attorney wanted some local jail time, but no prison, and for a limited time.

I thought we did very well. I know how these things go and it could have been far, far worse. I informed my client as to the entire picture and strongly suggested that he take the plea. However, my client refused to plead to that felony. He simply refused. The facts were not in our favor, and, as the court file suggests, bond conditions were violated while on bail. The County Attorney's Office considered my client dangerous to himself and others. I could not convince him to take the plea. In short, I was fired.

Ok, fine. No problem. Not the first time a client refused my advice. Not the first time I was discharged and replaced. You don't take that personally. The doctor finds another lawyer from the big city and decides to take the matter to a public trial. I'm sure his fee was exorbitant. His new lawyer made all sorts of assurances and said all those things the doctor wanted to hear. The case goes to a jury trial with his new, big city, pony-tail lawyer. The jury did not take awfully long to find him guilty on all counts. The former client was sentenced to two to four years in State Prison. There is a moral to this story. Always, always listen to old lawyers. They know the neighborhood. They know how it all works, and how it all ends up. They know the judges. Again, that lawyer went home to his wife and kids, pocketed the money he charged for his services. But the client doctor was taken to prison in a state vehicle.

As a footnote, the doctor called me several months later. That was an emotional conversation, I assure you. He wanted to tell me I was right, and he was wrong. He wanted to apologize. I did not do any "I told you so" comments. I told him to please stay in touch. His elderly mother also called a couple weeks later, crying her eyes out and telling me I was only looking out for her son's welfare, and that he should have heeded my counsel. His come to Jesus' moment came at the wrong place and at the wrong time. Too late now, wasn't it?

124

Perhaps, just perhaps, a lesson was learned. Sometimes you lose sleep over cases like this.

26
The Truth Sometimes Does Hurt

As I have written previously, family law cases are the worst of the worst. Even after a divorce, the parents, and the children must find a meeting ground and a way to all come together to give the kids a safe, loving, consistent, even a semblance of a stable family life. In this matter, the parents and the children could not find any common ground in which the children felt safe and both parents felt good and secure that the children were in good hands. I really disliked this case because it forced me to do things I hate to do, and that involve the children in the litigation.

The court records show that this matter revolved around two minor children in their teens who were subject to some abuse by their father. Without getting into details, the court file and the testimony at trial was that it was alleged that the two teenage girls were grabbed by the hair and yelled at in their faces, punched repeatedly and kicked, slammed against a wall, being hit causes bruises, etc. The eldest girl began to create self-inflicted cuts on top of her thighs, in a place that was not visible to her mom. The eldest daughter also began to exhibit anorexic tendencies and depression. It was also alleged that alcohol consumption by the father was a factor here.

The eldest daughter was taken to the clinic for an exam. A Sheriff's deputy arrived, interviewed the girl with a county Department of Family Services employee. They agreed that the children be placed in the custody of their mother until such time as the matter was investigated. It came to a point in which the girls refused to spend time with the father. It was at this time that I became involved. I advised that both parties need to go to counseling to help resolve their differences and to explore this alleged abuse by the father. Both parties went to as many as nine counseling sessions. The father would agree on a certain visitation schedule, then would renege on the agreement, and refuse to discuss any agreement whatsoever. The father wanted to leave the matter up to a judge.

I was eventually retained by the mother to secure a change in custody pursuant to a substantial change in circumstances due to the alleged abuse by the father. The father fought like hell in this case. An Answer was filed by the father with a Cross-complaint against the mother. The girls, on the other hand, felt a great deal of anxiety over going to court and their father's refusal to compromise. The father was adamant in his attitude. He would not budge. He had family who were lawyers and I believe this may have been a factor in his decision to fight. The father retained his family's law firm and presented to the Court two lawyers to defend this action. Everything a parent should not do for the sake of his children was done in this case.

We filed a complaint for a Modification of Custody and Visitation, for an Order that Defendant be ordered to seek counseling and take anger management classes and/or counseling, that Defendant not consume alcohol during any such visitations, and that Plaintiff the children remain in the care and custody of the Plaintiff until further order of the Court.

127

The father retained the wife's law firm. They fought tooth and nail on this case. The filed an Answer, a Cross complaint and proceeded to Discovery that took us months to sort out. They also filed motions for temporary custody, motions for Summary Judgement, motions to exclude evidence, motions in-limine, motions to admit expert witnesses, etc. It took months of litigation to get this matter to trial. I continued to do everything I could do to try and settle this matter, but to no avail. In the meantime, the girls suffered through it. Children always do in these cases.

The matter went to a full-on public trial. The trial took days of testimony, including the mother, father, the experts, officers, and the girls' testimony was taken in chambers, as is usually the case. In chambers, in the Plaintiff mother's case in chief, the girls testified that they were being physically abused by their father and described in detail what he had done and how he had hurt them. The judge listened intently, as counsel did. The Defendant's attorney cross examined the girls for some time, trying to catch an inconsistency or a lie. After the Defendant's counsel had finished her cross, she said the magic words, "no further questions." The judge asked, are the children excused? Yes, both parties: "they are excused."

When the plaintiffs' case was concluded, the Defendant took the witness stand. Defendant denied all that was said by their daughters. He stated that he had never harmed or hit them in any way. After his exam, the court went to a recess. It was my turn to cross-exam the father. I had previously asked my client to have the girls sit in the courtroom after their examination by Defendant's counsel, at a time when I was to cross examine their father. When the court reconvened, the girls sat in the courtroom audience section. Defendant's counsel objected to their attendance during the cross examination by me. The judge asked what the legal basis of the objection was. Defense counsel stated that it was improper as well as inappropriate to have the children present

128

during the cross examination of their father. I argued that the children had been excused from any testimony and that there was no legal basis for them to not view the proceedings. The judge agreed, and placed on record that the Court could find no legal basis as to their being removed since they were excused and overruled her objection. The children sat in the front row.

I kept asking questions about his daughters, how he had helped raise them, how they were doing in school, their behavior, and especially, their honesty. I asked him if he and their mother had taught them to be honest about all things. He answered in the affirmative. Also, I also asked why he thought that his lessons of honesty had been imbued into their character. He had nothing but praise for his daughters, a position I knew he would take. I then asked specifically how their daughters had lied about what they had testified before the court in chambers. Dead silence. He then stated that they did not lie as to anything they said. You could hear a pin drop in that courtroom. After my cross examination, and after my examination of the expert witnesses who counseled the children, I concluded my case in chief. Both parties made closing arguments to the court.

The Court did not take the matter under submission but made a decision from the bench. The Court found that there was a substantial change in circumstances to modify custody. The court said that the father's upbringing of the girls was detrimental to them to the point where there is a fear factor involved with both the children. The court changed custody to the mother and stated that that was in the best interests of the children. The court did grant visitation by the father every other weekend, with the visits with the youngest of the two. The eldest daughter, because of her issues of fear would have to start more slowly with counseling with the child counselor, then with dinner visits until the counselor deems it safe for overnight visits. We call that a gradual reintroduction with father and daughter.

The result of this matter was precisely what I had informed the opposing counsel would be done by the court. But to no avail. When you have credible allegations of abuse, especially from mature teenage children, the court will listen. The court will act, period. But instead, they chose to litigate this matter to death and create as much chaos within the family and the relationship with their children as they could. To the mother's credit she wanted to settle and did agree on terms of visitation, but the father refused. There were no other options available to my client and I but litigate. Sometimes you find yourself in a position you do not want to be in. I was forced into doing what I hate to do. But, if I had to do it, I was going to do the best I could for the mom and her children. Because under the circumstances I found myself in, it was the only thing I could do. Obviously, the Court agreed.

This matter was a garden variety, typical case in which litigation solves no problems, and makes the family dynamics far worse. The father will never again see his daughters the same way. He will always remember that the girls testified against him in a public open court. The girls too, will always remember that their father denied doing anything wrong, and thereby forcing them into that courtroom to testify against him. It was traumatic for both. The entire situation could have been resolved in mediation with honesty by the father as to his continued loss of temper with the girls and putting his girls first by listening to what they had to say in mediation.

I also place some responsibility on the stepmother and her lawyers, who, as legal counsel, should have known better than to force the judicial system to make an obvious choice when it certainly was unnecessary. They put those girls in an untenable situation. The mediation offer by the mother was far more advantageous to the father than the court's decision. It usually happens that way. The inability to accept the reality of your conduct sometimes has difficult and emotional consequences.

As a footnote, I was told by others that the relationship between the daughters and the father was patched up and in good shape. In sum, the father was a good man who needed to see what his girls needed and the stress they were experiencing. I was very glad to have heard that for the sake of the children a productive relationship was worked on and developed by the father. Children need a warm and loving relationship with both parents. In many cases both parents seem to forget that.

27
The Dirty Old Man

Despite the claim that sexual harassment in the workplace is a relatively new compensatory claim, it has been around since the Women's Christian Temperance Movement worked to protect women from harassment and coercion in the late 19th century. When I was starting out in the early eighties, we called it sexual assault, or intentional infliction of emotional distress, battery, and so on. It had always been a form of discrimination and a means by which women could sue for damages. The term "sexual harassment" did not come onto its own until the late the 1980's when the Supreme Court interpreted Title VII of the Civil Rights Act of 1964 to include discrimination based on "sex" as sexual harassment in the workplace. Over the years this form of harassment has taken on two forms, quid pro quo harassment (when a person in a position of power demands sexual favors) and hostile work environment harassment (unwanted sexual comments and behaviors).

This case came to me from a recommendation to the client from a relative of hers. She claimed she was sexually harassed in the workplace by a wealthy man, who had hired her as a caregiver. My client was a licensed Certified Nurse Assistant, CNA. She was reluctant to see me, she said, because she thought that since this employer was an elderly and very wealthy man and prominent in the community, she would be, in effect, banished from all employment in this town. She had recently moved here from another state and was wanting to start a new life, make friends, have a good career with a steady income.

How important was this man? He was a semi-retired Chairman of the Board of Directors of several large corporations that owned a chain of financial offices around the world, doing business to the tune of billions of dollars in assets. He was the then current member of a governmental commission for an eastern state; past director of the Association of Financial Holding Companies, was a board member of several colleges and universities. and received many honors and honorary degrees, throughout his life. He was a multi-millionaire. Wow! This guy doesn't even need to make a reservation in a good restaurant!

My client had told me a little as to what had occurred and that other employees were experiencing the same conduct but refused to come forward. My client was very reluctant to talk about the specifics as to what had happened to her. I didn't push it. However, I asked my client to be assessed by at least two medical professionals as to her emotional state. My client was diagnosed with acute stress disorder, with specific fear behavior after traumatic events. She exhibited frequent flashbacks, distress when exposed to triggers, negative moods, depression, anger, anxiety, and guilt. When I spoke to these health professionals they went on and on as to her symptoms and the damage she has suffered. She was not a young woman, but in her forties, and mother of three. She was genuinely traumatized by the conduct of this Dirty Old Man, hereinafter referred to as "DOM." When we were

133

together at my office, and talked about all the specifics, she cried a lot. Lawyer's love clients who cry.

My client was hired by this DOM as a personal caregiver. As a caregiver, she would bring him his meals, ferry him around town, shop for him, give him his medication, whatever was needed at any given time. When on duty, my client would dress for work, put her hair in a bun, wear slacks, and a jacket. She was told by this DOM to instead wear her hair down, short skirts, high heels. On two occasions, Mr. DOM reached out to grab her breasts, but his hands were pushed aside. He once grabbed her hand and placed it on his crotch, but she pulled away. She was called upon to go with him to Europe wherein he offered to give her a $1,000 bonus for spending money. After she declined the money, he stated it was a gift. He later said that "maybe I can get a little something in return." She tried to return the money, but he refused to accept it. After their return to Wyoming, the harassment continued. He dropped his pants to display his privates, pointed to her breasts "I ought to grab those, and so on, and so on.

The last straw for my client was while they were in Europe, the wealthy DOM was in a sitting room at the villa and was openly viewing child pornography on his personal laptop computer. I found that especially disturbing. What she saw disgusted her and will not be described here. The caregiver was not the only individual who was dismayed at his avocation. But his attitude was entrenched. "Everyone needs to shut the fuck up, because I don't give a damn, and I can do what the fuck I want to do." A very typical rich guy attitude toward life and everyone around them. I dislike those types of people.

This trip to Europe was the last straw. My client needed this job, she was paid very well, but she simply could not tolerate the constant sexual comments, fondling, assaults, and propositions. She left her employment. She spent weeks unable to sleep, in deep depression, with intrusive thoughts, a great deal of anger, and guilt.

Some lawyers would be reluctant to take on such a case. If things go bad, it could very well destroy your career. Do not think I am exaggerating, I'm not. I knew, this man would retain the absolute biggest and best law firm money could buy, and would seek to not only prevail, but destroy me and my reputation in the process. However, after spending a great deal of time with my client, I knew she was telling the truth. You must do your due diligence and make sure your client is sincere and was indeed damaged by the actions of any potential defendant. She was.

I prepared a civil complaint with the Wyoming District Court but, have not yet filed the action. I could have prepared a federal action and a complaint with the EEOC, knowing the time limitations involved. We held off, for the time being. Wyoming has its own similar statute regarding sex discrimination and harassment, and numerous common law remedies, such as intentional infliction of emotional distress, sexual assault, sexual battery, hostile work environment, and so on. We had a bit of time to decide in that regard. However, I must decide as to how I would proceed with this.

I believe most lawyers would have simply filed that complaint and let the chips fall where they may. By filing the lawsuit, not only would this wealthy DOM be the center of attention in the Wyoming media, be it newspapers, radio, or TV, but so would my client. That was the problem. Lawsuits are public. All information contained in the suits would be for public consumption. There would be no way for me to put the genie back in that bottle. Filing a suit like this may be the standard fare in the big city. It would be noticed, but not for long, if this case were filed in Los Angeles or San Francisco. I believe that most small town, rural lawyers here in Wyoming would have given their left testicle to have a case like this to hit the airwaves. Their futures would have been secure, with their name plastered all over the media for at least months, maybe years. And besides, everybody hates men who sexually harass women, and especially, the exploitation of children for sex!

However, I knew far too well that filing this suit here in a relatively small, rural, even upscale town, would cause quite a commotion. The potential defendant was far too public a person in his own right, was far too prominent in the community, in the state and the nation. It was a situation in which even the national newspapers would have grabbed the story. But the suit would also have the potential of putting my client on the front page of every newspaper in the state, and potentially, nationwide. In Los Angeles you can melt into the woodwork. Certainly not here. We discussed this possibility with my client. She cried. She begged me to find another scenario, another way to do this without putting her in the public eye to be examined and scrutinized.

I told her that there was another way to do this, but privately, but that if it fails, we must file that suit. This man's actions were so extraordinarily brutal to my client, so nefarious to her and to others unknown, that something had to be done. I have always hated bullies and those who believe they are wealthy enough, politically powerful enough, that they can do things that us common folk cannot do. After all, this is not DC! That was the situation here. After all, this was one of the reasons I worked so hard to become a lawyer. You know, save the innocent, the meek, the humble.

I decided to grab the bull-by-the-horns. I wrote a two-page letter directly to that DOM, describing in detail my client's allegations, and suggesting that he secure legal counsel. He most certainly did, and pronto. As predicted, within seven days I received a response from a prominent local firm. Of course, they denied all the allegations, every single one. But I was not deterred one bit. I knew something was going to happen, knowing that these lawyers were smart enough to know I was not bluffing, not going to go away. They were in a tricky, if not a delicate situation. They had to either tell me to go to hell or to somehow seek to nip this problem in the bud before it went public.

They communicated with me in that they thought we should talk before any action was filed. That to me meant that they had done their homework, had spoken to their client, and had spoken to other employees about our accusations. Obviously, despite their denials they knew that we were not either fabricating these stories or even exaggerating. They knew they had a problem. I only wish I could have been that fly on the wall to have heard what they discussed. However, I pretty much knew what they thought. The law firm knew that we were telling the truth. My client was not the only victim and that this bad conduct had gone on for quite some time with other women and no one in his family obviously either had the courage or the fortitude to stop it. I am sure they thought long and hard about the potential blowback from all of this. His reputation was such that he was thought of as a kindly, charitable, benevolent man who gave plenty of money to various causes and community activities.

The discussions with opposing counsel revolved around mediation of the problem with a neutral third party, but it had to be done soon. There are time limits on reporting sexual harassment with the Federal government and with the State EEOC. I was under a great deal of pressure on this case because of my client's refusal to take the matter public, and file the law suit I had prepared. If word of this came to light, I would be sunk, and my position would be compromised. Clients must be told the realities of the system, how the system works, the threat of a suit, and all it embodies and contains, the publicity that may happen. The Discovery process of confidential and private information must be explained in and out there and made known to your client. To us plaintiff's lawyers such a situation of confidential information unknown to the public is better than a wedge, it is a hammer that must be used on occasion. Without it, you have no cards to play. Sounds rather harsh, but it is what it is. I learned that in South Brooklyn.

We picked a neutral mediator that both sides could be happy with. He was a lawyer I knew quite well and was the opposing counsel in a contract dispute a few years earlier. I knew him to be fair and reality based. We considered a past governor as a mediator, but he turned it down since he knew the potential defendant. The mediator we picked was a veteran, a person of extensive experience. He was widely known in the legal community and respected. But most important of all was that he lived and worked a couple hundred miles away, and never met the DOM. I did not want a local mediator. Too close to the problem, too close to the potential defendant's reputation and connections.

Just prior to the mediation I asked the mediator that my client be kept a distance from the DOM. I did not want them to meet in a hallway even accidentally. My client was going through far too much emotional stress as it was. At the mediation table, when the mediator walked in, my client was already on the verge of tears. I could see it coming. Again, lawyers like clients who cry. Nothing, but nothing shows pain, emotion, distress like tears, nothing. Once your client starts crying, whether it is at a mediation, a deposition, you've got them. Your opponent never forgets that, and it will cement in his mind when the time comes to settle or take the matter to trial. The last thing your opponent wants to see is a plaintiff who cries on the stand, especially when he must cross examine them at trial.

At the mediation itself, it began well. The mediator made the usual speech to my client as to the advantages of a mediation versus a trial, the uncertainty of a trial, the usual. Although this case was different, I assured the mediator, since it was my opinion that if this case went to trial the punitive damages exposure to the defendant could be enormous. The mediator, nodded and said, "you may be right." I knew I had the near perfect case. I knew it, and the mediator knew it. All that needed to be done was to convince the opposition. It did not take long.

The mediator finished absorbing our position and moved on to the opposition. He came back with a five-figure offer, stating that my client was an employee for only a short period of time and that a jury would be hard put to award a great deal of money. I disagreed. It was not the length of the harassment but the quality of the harassment that is in issue. I simply said that if that is their best offer, I will file the suit tomorrow. The mediator gulped. Let me go back to them.

The mediator, after a discussion with the opposition came back with a six-digit offer. Still not good enough. I was convinced that if this matter went to trial my client would be awarded punitive damages. What this man did was disgusting and should be punished for it and to publicly tell the world that this kind of behavior will not be tolerated from anyone. I was prepared to argue that no one, not even a wealthy man in this community, who believed he "could do whatever he wanted," was immune to the law and to the ire of a jury of twelve country jurors. After some time spent at mediation, we had agreed on a multiple six figure settlement. I was satisfied, my client felt vindicated.

My only hesitation was that the community would never find out about this man and what he had done for so long, to so many. As you can guess, there was a non-disclosure provision (NDA) in the settlement agreement. Of course, they insisted upon it. My client readily agreed since she wanted no one to know if she was even involved in this for the sake of her future employment. I was compelled to agree.

What bothered me the most was that at the mediation he was accompanied by other women employees that knew what he was doing, when he was doing it, and to whom he was doing it too. These women were not hayseeds. They were world wise and savvy. They knew the entire story of this DOM, and his history. They should have known better then to have tolerated that sort of conduct to other women. However, they looked the other way. They did nothing about it and said nothing for many years. The why was simple to figure out. They wanted to keep their high paying jobs and were willing to sacrifice other women for their income, and their own purposes. So much for the 'Me Too' movement. Sometimes the wealthy and the powerful do live on a different tier of justice. I have seen it all too often. We all see it every day with politicians and those in power. It's terribly unjust and is an insult to our basic precepts of equal protection of the laws whether it be for the wealthy or in politics. What is infuriating is that sometimes we look the other way and let them. They just get away with it.

As a footnote, the DOM passed away a short two years after this matter was settled. I sure hope he asked for forgiveness to the powers that be for his past conduct.

28

When Government Drops a Lead Ball on Your Foot

This case came to me by a panic-struck phone call. "My niece is in jail, my niece is in jail, please help!" Ok, ok, what's the problem? I was told that her niece was arrested via an arrest warrant for failure to present to the State Employment Workforce Division her payroll records for a childcare business she owned about six years prior. How can that be? She was arrested on a six-year-old arrest warrant. Wow! Talk about a stale case and right to speedy trial issue.

I went to see her personally in jail the following morning. What I found was a nice lady, about 40 years old. She told me that she thought that her other aunt, who owned the business, had submitted the requested payroll records to the Workforce Division years ago. But the business was closed six years ago. You didn't own that business, I asked? "No, I did not, my aunt owned the business. But my name was on the license as a co-owner." I asked whether she knew for sure whether her aunt submitted those payroll records. She told me she thought she had but wasn't sure. I asked, "don't the two of you tell each other what is going on?" She said that she and her aunt do not speak to each other at all, that there is some bad blood between the two of them.

I made some phone calls to other relatives and found that the records were indeed sent to the Workforce Division some six years prior. I was a bit incensed by this since my client had been in jail for three days for no damn good reason, and that it did not take me long to find out what was going on and who did what to whom. It seemed to me that the aunt should have stepped in to clear the air as to what was going on. I immediately called the court to have the case placed on the calendar for a quick hearing the next day.

At the hearing I argued that the case was far too stale, and that we can prove that the payroll records were submitted. The Assistant Attorney General apologized for their mistake and admitted that the records were indeed given to the Department years ago, but that someone in their department was in error. I was not very understanding at all by this explanation, and refused to accept the apology, since if the Attorney General's office knew the records were submitted, they should have informed the court immediately of the error and released my client. But they did not and waited days to inform the court! I was able to discover all the facts of this matter in only a few hours. The State Attorney General's Office had the case for six years. Somebody dropped the ball, and big time.

The judge was not happy about all of this. Especially since I informed the court that my client had lost her job over this incarceration. The judge, being the conscientious and judicious man that he is, offered to call her employer to explain the situation. The Court, not wanting to wait for a written formal dismissal in the coming days, issued a hand-written order for her release and for the case to be dismissed with prejudice right then and there with a formal apology.

Never assume documentary and testimonial facts issued by the powers of the state or federal governments are true because sometimes they are not. They do make mistakes. Not often, but they do happen. My client insisted the State of Wyoming was wrong, and sure enough, they were. My client thanked me for getting her out of jail and for a successful resolution. She asked for a bill for my services. I told her no bill would be forthcoming. She had suffered enough already. There are times when being a grunt trial lawyer has rewards you cannot put a price on!

29

SF 104 Case, or The Senate File from Hell

Because of the small population and low density of people in Wyoming, to attract hundreds of people to any event in your very small town is rather remarkable in itself; since the state, as large as it is, has half the population of metro Richmond, Virginia, or of Sacramento, California. The result will shock local farmers and ranchers who have never seen that many people in one place. You come to realize that with large crowds of people you inevitably attract politicians, and plenty of them.

These events were organized to give the locals the opportunity to meet and greet their own representatives. As stated previously, my backyard (large in acres) welcomed three U.S. Senators, two congressmen, a future governor, candidates, and many state representatives. Media by-the-score attended, including the Boston Globe, USA Today, Billings Gazette, even a reporter from the London Daily Telegraph attended! (The London reporter was amazed at the expanse of the western landscape!) I can only guess that since it was an election year, when opponents attend the same event, the reporters hope something juicy happens.

The SF-104 fiasco was an offshoot of these events. At this time, we had an embattled State Superintendent of Public

Instruction having a disagreement with the Governor. In Wyoming, our Superintendent was elected by the people and had been since 1890, when the state Constitution was ratified. Our Constitution was quite specific as to the powers and duties of the Superintendent. In short, the Constitution provides that "The general supervision of the public schools shall be entrusted to the state superintendent of public instruction, whose powers and duties shall be prescribed by law."

On or about January 2013, the Governor stripped the Superintendent of her official duties on grounds she did not manage the department properly and created a "hostile working environment." Many of us believed it was more of a power play by the Governor and some state senators as to the education of the children. This Superintendent was different from others in the past, in that she moved the focus of the state office in Cheyenne from data collection and compliance to federal guidelines to a concentration on the improvement of public instruction. What a concept! Worthy goals.

However, old guard legislators only want changes that might increase their power and influence. This new emphasis was a threat. They drafted a bill to transfer the responsibilities, funding, and personnel from the Superintendent's office to the State Board of Education. Thus, the infamous SF-104 bill was born.

The legislature soon passed the final bill, which was signed by the Governor. A coup had been undertaken, destroying a constitutionally created state office, thereby silencing the voters. A suit was filed to contest the law, arguing that the change could only be voted through an amendment to the state Constitution, a difficult task at best. A legal team representing the Superintendent was created. I was picked as part of that team. Since I dislike any political move that takes power from the people, I accepted. Besides, I worked for free.

The Governor claimed he did not violate the Constitution, that SF-104 was perfectly valid and challenged the suit. The state Attorney General was the lead counsel that opposed us. In the interim, the Governor contracted with an out of state politician to be the newly created "Education Director." As a footnote, he was paid far more than the Superintendent!

As part of the legal team, it was my position that the constitutional provision and its original meaning which created the position of superintendent was violated. Call me an originalist. That is, if you can reinterpret any constitutional provision by twisting, turning, distorting, deviating, or bending words to fit your political agenda, then no constitutional provision is safe. The result is that no liberty or franchise that is protected by that provision is safe from government intrusion. All that was needed, I thought, was to argue that the founders, which created the office of public instruction, meant exactly what they wrote in the Constitution at its founding, by its plain meaning. What was done, to my eyes, was to craft a legal argument that took apart the provision, word by word, and that it be particularly defined through its dictionary meaning, as it was understood by the creators back in 1890.

Since the Constitutional provision of Art. 7 Section 14 of the Wyoming Constitution contains only twenty-six words, only four of those words needed to be defined. I provided to the Supreme Court in that brief a dictionary meaning to only four words: general; supervision; entrusted; superintendent. I believe that argument contained less than ten pages when you take apart Art. 1, Sec. 14 to only four critical words. There was a case law basis for my argument since I found the Supreme Court did such a thing in a case years before.

"It cannot be that simple," as was inferred by others on the team! But yes, it can, said, this grunt lawyer. I have always found that quite often the simplest arguments are the most effective. The remaining three arguments, which occupied the great bulk of the brief, were prepared by others on the team. However, the Court did not even consider those arguments since eventually they found SF-104 unconstitutional on that ground alone, the original meaning of the founders!

After the suit was filed, it was well known in the legal community that I was a member of that team challenging that new law. In spring of 2013, I attended a state political convention in Cheyenne. Of course, the Governor was in attendance as was I. As it were, he was looking for me, as I was looking for him to say hello, and mend fences. In the past we had been quite friendly with each other, having helped him get elected. I liked the man. He was easy to talk to. The Governor did find me through the large crowd and asked to speak to me in private. That doesn't sound good. We left the main ballroom and went into the hall. After the pleasantries, he explained his decision to sign the bill, telling me his legal team and his Attorney General insisted the bill was constitutional. That set me off since the Governor had been a U.S. Attorney for twenty some odd years, and should have known better, since the provision was so clear. I also said that what was being done by some politicians was an end run around the amendment process. He certainly did not like that. It ended with a yelling match, which some people heard outside the door in the convention hall. These people were listening in on the conversation and heard the conflict. This can't be good. One deputy county attorney who overheard the conversation made such a comment in my presence.

I now believed I could be a target. A large state like Wyoming with a very small population has a very close legal community. But so-what. I was just entering retirement age.

What could they possibly do to me? There is nothing like having the Governor of your state publicly yelling at you for taking an opposite position on a very big change in legislation. Not exactly a career boost! But older lawyers are harder to push around.

I found out about the Supreme Court's decision early in the morning on a weekday. The Wyoming Supreme Court in a majority opinion ruled that the SF-104 legislation was unconstitutional. I was delighted. I had a court appearance that day, so we were more concerned with preparation for the appearance in a criminal matter. Upon entering the court room, it was filled with other lawyers waiting for their case to be called. The presiding judge entered the court room, and to my surprise, mentioned to all in the court that the legal team of which I was part, had prevailed before the Wyoming Supreme Court in the celebrated, yet infamous, SF 104 debacle. All in the court room stood up and applauded. It was one of the most gratifying moments of my career. Since I was never paid for the contribution, and never asked to be paid, it was still well worth the effort. Money becomes meaningless when you fight for what you believe in. It all ended well and became a shining moment in my career.

30

A Word About Intoxicated Driving Cases

I have probably handled hundreds of drunk driving cases, both in California and Wyoming. The drunk driving case described in Chapter Four was just a small sample of the cases I have seen that involved an over-indulgence of alcohol. Drunk driving or DUI (driving under the influence) cases are not what they used to be. Back when I started my law practice the courts were far more lenient than they are now. With the inception of organizations such as Mother Against Drunk Driving (MADD), the courts, and the state legislators, have become tougher on those who drink and drive. Drunk drivers account for thousands of deaths each year. The penalties for DUI driving have become increasingly more onerous for those who are convicted. The blood alcohol level for conviction has dropped over the years from .10 to .08.

The one unique thing about DUI cases is that it can happen to anyone, to any of us. One Superior Court Judge in California once told me that the only thing that separated us from the DUI defendants was that "they got caught, and we didn't." How true that is. Most of us, if we are honest about it all, will admit to drinking more than was prudent at any given time. But make no mistake, a DUI conviction on your record will assure a sharp spike in your auto insurance rates, and a review by your local state motor vehicle department as to whether they wish to suspend your driver's license. The courts have no jurisdiction over the state motor vehicle department, on what they do and not do regarding the status of your driving privileges. Your lawyer cannot help you there.

Most of my DUI cases were simple first-time offenders who had just a little too much to drink. Most blew anywhere from a .08 to a .12 on the breath machine. These breath machines are generally accurate but not entirely and can be affected by anything from operator error to lack of maintenance. The most accurate is always the blood test. Most lawyers will ask for maintenance records of these machines to determine accuracy and proper use. The blood test - well, it is what it is. I had one client who tested a .23 BAL. That is an extremely high BAL, nearly three times the legal limit. I could not understand why it was so high since I did not believe she drank enough for the level to be so high. I later found that she had gastric bypass surgery several years before. We lawyers love it when a client has a physical condition that will always artificially read a false high BAL. I proved to the DA that such surgery will elevate the BAL to as much as 40% due to the gastric bypass rather than the actual amount of alcohol she may have consumed. Instead of a jail sentence she received a deferral, or a dismissal after six months of clean behavior. A good result.

Then there are those who never learn, never correct their behavior. I had a client with a .26 BAL on a fifth DUI charge. This guy was incorrigible. A real habitual drinker with anger problems. His father retained me to represent him. His father impressed me as a man who has had a chronic drinking problem himself over the years. He was very thin, drawn, unshaven, and with a less than accommodating personality. I told him that this would be a tough case. Not only was his son caught with a high BAL but that was only a small part of the matter. When he was stopped by the CHP (California Highway Patrol) for speeding, the cop, as usual, got out of the car to speak to the driver. The client then took off at a high rate of speed and led the CHP on a chase down the highway for 20 miles at 90 plus mph. The man was charged with felony drunk driving, resisting arrest, assault on an officer, etc. This is one of those cases in which a lawyer can do little except assure that your client's rights are protected. After five priors, an exceedingly high BAL, a car chase, resisting arrest, the DA and the court had enough of this guy. They threw the book at him. He was sentenced to eighteen months in prison. After the sentencing, the father looked at me and said: "this is all your fault!" It was then that I knew why this client was the way he was. Way too much enabling by the parents, and much guilt for less than commendable role models.

When all the facts are against you, when the priors are numerous, when it seems impossible to create a miracle, and when it seems there are few mitigating factors and many aggravating factors, all you can do is make sure your client's rights are protected. When the client blames the lawyer, you cannot permit that to get you down. Do the best you can and that is it. It is what it is. Let it go. One of the low points of being a lawyer. You cannot take it home. Easier said than done.

The Wyoming attitude towards DUI cases is a bit different and somewhat more forgiving than they are in California. I knew a man who was intoxicated while riding his horse, rode up to an old and famous local hotel, went through the front door, screaming "yahoo!" until he was felled by hitting his head on an exit sign! Alcohol has a different, if somewhat more romantic reputation than in the cosmopolitan cities. You can buy alcohol in a drive through liquor store, and even order a mixed drink! Although the standard of .08 BAL is the same in both states, the fines are much higher in California than they are in Wyoming. California is more apt for you to spend a little time in the county jail for a high BAL than Wyoming.   I never had a client spend time in jail, other than the initial arrest, in Wyoming, for a simple DUI. This goes for all clients I have had, whether their BAL was .10 through .24. No such luck in California. But then again, Wyoming, as in most states, is not tolerant of repeat offenders.

31
COURT CLERKS

Court clerks and judges' assistants are the unwritten heroes of the justice system. The courts cannot live without them. They maintain court records, file the paperwork you ask to be filed, present the court files to you for your review, schedule hearing and trial dates, distribute orders of the court, and are the best conduit between you and the judge. If they like you, they will let you use their copy machines and staplers. They will tell you if a motion or other paperwork has been filed. They will even inform the judges what in the world is going on in a case. In short, they provide support to the judges, the attorneys, and other officers of the court. Most importantly, they would inform you if you screwed something up.

During hearings, they will be there and sit through all your mundane, boring sometimes nonsensical arguments to the court. I knew one court clerk that struck the fear of God in all lawyers in that court. Lord help you if you were late, or if you failed to mark an exhibit, or if you failed to sign a document. I will never forget the look you received. I have seen veteran lawyers simply melt into mush by that look of disdain. That clerk made a better lawyer of me. Yes, on many occasions, I just sat there and took it all. I have known that clerk for 40 years. And to this day is a good and respected friend.

A word of advice to all new lawyers. Get on their good side. They will make or break your practice. Never make the mistake that you think you know more than they do. Trust me on this, you do not. Having a good relationship with the court clerks may even save your bacon, as it were. The best example of their importance is this anecdote. Many years ago, while preparing a brief in a case in which I had a poor relationship with an argumentative and quarrelsome opposing counsel, my secretary and I started playing and joking with the brief by referring to the opposing attorney as an "asshole." Of course, we had no intention of filing such a brief, but we were having fun with it for a laugh. Laughter is a great stress reliever.

I cannot tell you how this happened, or by what means it happened, but that word was still in the brief in several places when it was filed! We received a phone call from the clerk of the court asking if we really intended to file such a paper with the court. My secretary asked why and was told as to the descriptive language in the brief. There was horror and panic in my office! To make a long story short, that brief was immediately replaced by a corrected version. That clerk saved my career. Be kind to them, gifts at Christmas may help.

32

A Word About Judges

Wow, now that's the topic that could get me in trouble! I have appeared in 14 different counties in California, six different counties in Wyoming, one county in Nevada, and one in Montana. I have appeared before judges that were White, Black, Hispanic, women, men, young, old, conservative, and liberal. When I first appeared in Court, I must admit I was awed by the judges. They made me extremely nervous, even scared me at times. Naturally after all these years, I no longer feel that way. An older lawyer that helped me was a wise sole. He told me that "these people are like anyone else, no better, no worse." "Just follow one into a bathroom, they stink and make the same horrid sounds as anyone else." I will never forget that advice. In fact, it helped quite a bit.

Judges are of many types, characters, personalities, sensibilities, and belief systems. There are judges you want to appear before, and those you would rather have a splinter removed from an infected and swollen finger. Some judges are humorous and try to make a difficult situation easier to deal with, and those that have not an ounce of whimsey. I know of judges who are pompous, with a severe and grim sense about them, and those that have a light air about them and will always try to find something good and hopeful to say. There are judges with a well-developed sense of humor and there are judges with none. I have known judges who you will never see smile and those that will always have a humorous anecdote to share. I have always preferred the latter. They make the practice of law far easier. A Wyoming judge I knew and admired, would always make a comment on my being a "California Lawyer." He made us all laugh.

Judges, like us lowly lawyers, also become jaded and difficult to deal with. One judge I knew, early in my career, became, over the years, intolerant of lawyers who took up too much of his time on the bench. He would always ask the time they needed for their argument and would always hold them to it. You see, lawyers know that the court will ask the lawyer the estimate of time to argue. This brief time estimate for argument always went first. Thus, lawyers would underestimate their time before the bench with hopes to get in and out of court before other lawyers. After repeated under-estimates of time, this judge purchased a gong and hammer and placed it on his bench. After the time estimate was up, he hit that gong, and that was it. End of argument. After several times hitting that gong, the lawyers all became more realistic as to their time estimates. I think the judge was inspired by the "Gong Show" popular back then. I'm really showing my age.

Another judge I knew and appeared before numerous times could be down-right nasty on the bench. I had a dispute with a Deputy DA as to the admissibility of evidence in a case. I believed that the stop and detention was improper and had no probable cause. The DA believed otherwise. I filed a Fourth Amendment motion to suppress the evidence gathered at the stop and detention, and a motion to dismiss for lack of evidence. We both argued about the motion. The judge seemed a bit off during the argument. You can tell. After the arguments, the judge looked at the Deputy and yelled at him "don't you believe in the Constitution?!" The judge then simply walked off the bench without a verbal ruling. We were both stunned and speechless. The Deputy was embarrassed. We looked at each other, and after a moment of quiet, I said to the Deputy, not knowing what else to say: "I guess I win this one." The judge was having a bad day. The case was dropped by the District Attorney's Office.

There is one judge I came to admire quite a bit. He always had a word of encouragement to anyone who came before the bench. He was always scrupulously fair and tried to be of help to all who came before him and would go above and beyond. He has that one quality all judges should have but few possess, and that is compassion and humility. This Judge was the product of many years of private practice, in both criminal and civil cases. He had a great deal of experience and knew the ups and downs of the practice of law and of life in general. He had a remarkably well-developed sense of humor who eased the nerves of any who appeared before him. Most importantly, he cared a great deal about the lawyers in this small county. He was called, and rightfully so, "the dean of the county lawyers." We had lawyers with persistent alcoholism, and chronic problems with the practice of law, etc. He helped them all. He was always there for advice.

The older judges are more self-confident. They know the road they travel on. And some who are new on the bench, ask in chambers for help from the attorneys that appear before them. Some retired judges will continue to appear in certain cases, if need be, when asked by the Judicial Counsel. I knew one older judge who started to nod out during a hearing. I knew another judge who, no matter what I said, went in one ear and out the other. This judge ruled in favor of a motion for summary judgment against my client and took the safe route in favor of the big law firm that appeared with their motion. I insisted that my opponent's motion was incorrect, but to no avail. Since such a ruling effectively ended my case,

157

I appealed. The Court of Appeals ruled that I was right, and the judge's ruling was clearing wrong. The case was settled. Beware of judges who habitually rule in favor of the big firms, and the Armani suits. In the 'fat lady case" in Chapter Eight Above, I did see the trial judge in an elevator after the Los Angeles Appeals Court ruled against him. He was embarrassed to be sure and said to me "I knew something was not quite right." Judges hate, that is hate, to be overturned by an appeals court. It is kind of like getting a bad report card in school. Nothing like a public display of all your mistakes.

There are judges who shoot from the hip, and there are judges who are incredibly detailed and scrupulous. In a rural county in California there were two Superior Court judges in the county. These judges could not be so different. One was quick to judge and rule, the other was very deliberate and careful. In time the lawyers began to categorize them as in one you will get a ruling without a rationale, and in the other a rationale without a ruling. Or as one lawyer put it: " forever reasoning without a decision, or you get a decision without a reason."

The secret here is to "know your judge." Know his/her values, characteristics, likes, dislikes, political affiliation, clubs, or organizations he/she may have an affinity for. Knowing your judge may just give you that leg up at trial. Let me give you an example. I had a client who purchased a motel. The seller made certain oral and written representations concerning the income and condition of the motel. My client was a recent immigrant from India. He brought his entire family with him to the motel to help him run the business. The problem was that none of the representations by the sellers were true. The property had hidden problems. The income records were falsified. The sellers were arrogant and cocky and had retained a well-respected lawyer who was under consideration for a judgeship. The seller kept declaring that "my lawyer is better than your lawyer, he's going to be a judge." Whatever. I knew the judge assigned to the case was very thorough and fair. I also knew he had spent several vacations in India and heard him speaking about the trip in glowing terms to others. Ok. He likes India, and Indians. He admires them and their culture. I kept that knowledge in my pocket. I asked my client to have his family sit in court during the trial. After all, I am up against this candidate for the bench. I needed to even up the odds. After three days in trial, the judge ruled in our favor, gave us everything we asked for and then some. He even awarded us attorney fees. Did my tactic work? Cannot say it did, cannot say it did not. But I believe it may have helped.

Most lawyers will appear before the same judge repeatedly. You cannot help but understand who and what impresses him. Some judges have poker faces, and you will never know what they are thinking. Some judges are more transparent and will, without thinking, instinctively nod in approval as you present your argument. Most of all, I have seen that most judges, if not all, want you to keep it simple. Simplicity is a gift a lawyer can give to a judge. Judges have many cases on the calendar and just not enough time to navigate complex and esoteric arguments. I remember one judge, after hearing arguments in a complex matter tell the lawyers to keep it simple. He must have said three times, "I am a simple man." I believe he liked my arguments because I am a very simple grunt lawyer, wearing a Macy's suit. You can always tell if a judge likes your arguments. He greeted my simple presentation like a breath of fresh air in a stuffy room. The motion I presented was won. The lesson to be learned: keep it simple. The judges will love you for it.

Be careful about appearing in a strange court you know nothing about. This is a new forum. You don't know the ropes. You don't know the judge. You must know that the DA, or County Attorney has appeared there on a regular basis, probably for years. He/she knows the judge, probably quite well. That is a distinct advantage you must try to overcome. In a recent case I had as pro hac in Montana, I retained two psychologists in a combat veteran criminal case. The evaluations were most certainly to our advantage and recommended no jail time, no treatment. We gave that County Attorney the evaluations so we could commence discussions on a disposition. He represented that he reviewed both evaluations. We could not agree on anything. The time came for a two-day sentencing hearing about a year later. Several days before the hearing, after arrangements for a hotel, plane tickets, subpoenaed witnesses, cost of expert witnesses, the County Attorney asked for a continuance to retain their own expert for an evaluation, stating he did not agree with our experts' evaluations! You're kidding me! He has had those evaluations for over a year and only now does he question their thoroughness?! It became apparent he did not review any of our expert evaluations. I was not happy about this since my client's money was not being well spent and would cost him dearly. We filed an opposition to the continuance in no uncertain terms and argued lack of diligence on the part of the State. The judge gave him the continuance in any case with no sanctions for such a late request! And why not? Once the case is over I'm gone. The County Attorney will be there the next morning! Please note, after the third evaluation it was found the new evaluator basically agreed with my psychologists! What do they say about Karma?

I have always liked judges. But some, more than others. When I was a young lawyer, I often used judges as mentors. How often I would try to convince them of the wisdom of my arguments. Now that I am past retirement age, they actually listen. Some judges are quite philosophical in their decisions, and some are just, well...decisive. The older you get and the more experience you have the easier it will become in your relationship with judges. Most respect age and time on the battlefield. One of the few advantages of being an old lawyer. Some understand what it takes to be a grunt in the trenches. They should. Most have been there almost as long or longer than I have. In one incident, I was in chambers with a District Court Judge, who had certainly been around the block. This judge I knew quite well when he was a lawyer. His behind the bench attitude and compassion for people made him to my mind one of the best judges I had known over these many years. He was always fair, always judicious, and never permitted his emotions to get out of line. There were times when the case load was over-bearing, and you could see the weariness on his face. He was almost as tired as I was. We spoke of inane topics. The time came to go to court and confront the issues to be presented there. He said to me: "Rob, let's get this over with and pretend we care." LOL. Lawyers are not the only officers of the court that experience burnout.

Afterthoughts

Climbing Out of the Trench on the Eve of Retirement

On the eve of retirement, do I have any regrets in my "life choice?" Having regrets is a mental exercise. All real conscientious, well-adjusted people have regrets about something or other. But having regrets can be such a waste of time since there is little you can do to change the things you regret you did. You can only learn from your regrets in your future conduct. Do I have any regrets? Sure. Probably more than most. I can even be accused of dwelling on them. But remember, as Ingrid Bergman once said: "happiness is good health and a bad memory."

I never regretted leaving Brooklyn, even though I missed it at times. Maybe it was the Italian food? But you can learn a great deal about life when you relocate to other regions. You learn about what other people think and why they think the way they do. Their perspectives become clear. Great learning experiences.

But most importantly, the opportunities you can be presented with are far more numerous when you allow yourself to open so many new doors. Unless I had moved out of Brooklyn, I don't think I would have had the opportunity to get an education I so desperately wanted, the chance to go to law school, and the chance to write about my own future. I saw an open door and ran, not walking through it. When I hear others tell me our American culture and system has limited opportunities or hear politicians or pundits tell us they cannot make it, that the institutions will work against them, I cringe. The opportunities we have here are virtually limitless. Ask the millions trying to get here. But it all depends on you, not them. Never put your life, your future, in the hands of others, or accept a defeatist opinion as gospel.

If you do you will have already lost. You will lose whatever initiative you have left. Get out there! A rocker friend of mine said, "all you need is a dream, a goal, and an alarm clock." If you are disappointed, learn from it, pick yourself up, then try again somewhere else. You will make it. I know this from experience.

No, I have no regrets about my "life choice." It was hard at times, awfully hard. But, since I was presented with the opportunity, I held onto it with both hands and feet. As a lawyer these so many years, I regret having taken on some client's problems as if they were my own. That will kill you. I regret coming home in a bad mood because of what lawyers, clients and sometimes judges had done to promote their own self-interest. I got annoyed when some silly young lawyer would not permit a valuable MFCC's report to be admitted into evidence in a child custody case because she believed the referral by the court was improper! I regret using a four-letter word when a judge who had a major conflict of interest in a case refused to recuse himself. I regret becoming upset when a prosecutor took himself too seriously, would not lighten up, and made it all personal! I should not have gone ballistic and got hot under the collar when a client, despite all my repeated warnings, refused to shut up when he was cross-examined! I often detested having to take a child custody matter to trial because the parents refused to compromise and put the kids first! There is just so much you can do to prevent nonsense. You just must deal with it and do the best you can.

You have no power over what other people say or do. But you do have power as to how it will affect your life and to those you love. It has taken me years to put it all under control since the only thing you can control is yourself and your life. A trial lawyer must buck up and take the heat and not take it home. Lawyers who take it home daily will either not be lawyers very long or will look for yet another Mrs. so and so.

There is such a thing as lawyer burnout. Make no mistake, burnout is real. It is when you have been mentally scorched by the legal system and your "life choice." Lawyers burn themselves out when after so many years of sometimes brutal verbal combat they start to lose their temper, become irritated by silly client questions, begin to stare at the ceiling during hearings, forget the wife's birthday, and generally astral project, or engage in other out-of-body experiences. Burnout is a real problem, especially with sole practitioners. It is the result of long hours, an unforgiving court calendar and justice system, an impersonal culture, endless numbers of people with endless problems. You do not experience burnout in one incident, but, rather, it is a long slow process of disconnection with family, friends, and health needs. It is chronic fatigue that manifests itself in far too many demands and increasingly fewer resources to deal with them. It is when you experience this cynicism about life that nothing you are doing is really changing the lives entrusted to you. When you start having panic attacks, experiencing irritability, anger, a sense of hopelessness, and those sharp pains in the chest, then you know that you must make major changes. You know that something needs to be done, and fast.

One of the lessons I have learned is that a lawyer cannot save the world. You are not Jesus or Mother Teresa. But you should understand that many of us have done a great deal of good for a great number of people. We have changed many

164

lives for the better. Come to that realization. It will lessen your stress. Try not to dwell on mistakes or miscalculations. That will kill you. Everyone makes mistakes, especially judges! Recognize your own personal symptoms of stress and burnout. We all know when we are being pushed to the edge.

Most of all, take a break, a long one of you can. Or at least slow down the practice. Don't take that case where the opposing attorney is a known knotty individual. It may be that at these times you must take a long vacation. If you cannot do that, then at least get involved in hobbies, or sports, or at least take the time to get reacquainted with your wife and kids. Get a medical exam and listen to your doctor.

I had one major burnout after that murder case, and after the "fatal attraction" case was concluded. Bad burnout. I was a basket case. I even thought of letting it all go and becoming a history teacher. Too much at stake. We packed up the pickup and the horse trailer and went to Wyoming and stayed on a working cattle ranch for ten days. It helped a lot. Clutching a new-born calf to place in the back of a pickup truck, while being chased by an infuriated mother cow in the middle of nowhere can pour water on a lot of flames in your incendiary attitude.

There are times I question the system that we have developed over these many hundreds of years, and our reputations that have followed that system. For the most part the system involves millions of people doing the best they can under sometimes difficult circumstances. Can it be improved? Of course, it can. We have an adversarial system of justice that has developed over hundreds of years of trial and error. It works well in criminal and civil law when the truth must be uncovered for justice to prevail. Each side is better served when they employ the lawyer with the proverbial baseball bat to compel the truth. It allows both parties to present their case through evidence, documents, and witnesses to support their positions, to a judge and/or a jury that has been chosen and examined for their impartiality. So long as you remember that your suit (from Armani or Macy's) is, in effect, full combat gear. If you don't forget that, you will survive.

However, I have never been happy about the family law aspect of my practice, and the system I must contend with as it relates to the children in issue. The adversarial approach sets up a system where each side is required to contest with each other as if in a civil case, such as wrongful death, personal injury, or breach of contract, where the parties are if not enemies, then pretty darn close. In family law matters I do not believe the parties should be placed in a position to view each other as enemies. They already feel that way, and it should not be reinforced by the courts. Far too much contention, far too little concern for the children and their welfare, by far too many lawyers is the end product. I see the system as confused and in the dark on this issue. The adversary system does not work well with children, and never will. It only increases the animosity the parties already feel about each other. The children will never forget the time when they had to go to court to speak to the judge in chambers as to which parent they preferred to live with, to the prejudice of the other. Families and the children would be better served by removing the source of the increased animosity, and treating the issues with calm and deliberate solutions to the problems by those who are trained to deal with the emotions and resolve these family issues. Never forget that whether it be a divorce or child custody matter it is a lawsuit. And as accurately stated by Janet Malcolm: "A lawsuit is to ordinary life what war is to peacetime. In a lawsuit, everybody on the other side is bad. A trial transcript is a discourse in malevolence."

That is why I am a great believer in mediation as the solution to these problems. Mediators who are specifically educated and trained to handle these custody/visitation matters are in a far better position to analyze the problem and help the parties reach an amicable solution that protects the minor children from the stress of the family break up and the stress of litigation. These men and women can reach solutions that are in the best interests of the children. Mediation should not be merely suggested by the courts, it should be required before any case is heard. I believe most cases would be resolved without litigation and without wasted court time. There would be that side benefit in that courts and judges could best be spending more time and resources on the overworked criminal justice system.

The family law legal system has become an industry like any other. Perhaps that is the problem. Those within it want to protect their income and their careers. In a county I know of and have practiced in, the court set up a system in which trained personnel would investigate parents and children in child custody matters to make recommendations to the court as to what the problem is, and how it can be solved. The court would order that a case be referred to them for investigation. Sure enough, many lawyers challenged and objected to these referrals as being "unconstitutional" and refused to cooperate. Not wanting to challenge these objections, the court simply asked for that lawyer's "permission" to refer the case! How absurd, and how detrimental to the families and the children involved! In my view, these lawyers certainly did not want a quick resolution to the problem. That would certainly cut into their income. These mediation referrals are especially challenged by younger lawyers. This is one of the times I have been embarrassed by my own profession. A great deal of reform is needed here.

Lawyer's reputations in our American culture and the public perception of us is the biggest disappointment I have as to my "life choice." It is not particularly good, to say the least. I was approached by an old lady in church one morning. The lady said to me "I hear you are a liar. I mean Lawyer." I said nothing. I will never forget that. I thought about that confrontation by that little old lady for years afterward. It cannot be denied by fair-minded people that the status of lawyers needs improvement. I have seen far too little concern about the reputation of lawyers in both the California State Bar and the Wyoming State Bar, and even lessor concern for most lawyers. If you ask a lawyer or a judge about it, they will simply shrug their shoulders.

Perhaps lawyer reputations could be improved if they did more volunteer work and went out of their way to solve problems rather than exacerbate them. In fact, exacerbating problems is what lawyers specialize in. It is what they do best. Trust me on this. I have seen it happen far too often. I was such a fan of mediation in family law cases that I tried to get a group of lawyers together to volunteer to mediate family disputes, for no cost. I sent out a letter, in that regard, to all lawyers I knew of in several counties. I received only one positive response to my request! Just one! Shameful.

Barristers in the United Kingdom are a different story, and have a much better reputation and, one would say, even celebrated. As described above, when I was in London, at the "Old Bailey" Court House to observe a criminal rape trial, the barristers invited me to lunch. Of course, in London the barristers have their own dining room. The judges, or "Lordships," have their own separate dining room. Their dinnerware is a lot nicer. As most people know, barristers wear wigs. Wigs go back hundreds of years and are symbols of an aristocratic breed. Prior to the revolution our lawyers wore them as well. It was the break with Britain that changed our aristocratic garb from a pretentious to a more common man. Anyway, at lunch one barrister, named Victor, removed his wig. I could not help but notice that there was what appeared to be a linen hanky sewed inside the wig. I could not help but ask him why that hanky was sewed inside the wig. He told me his wife had sewed it in there several years ago. "Why was that?" I asked. He began to tell the history of that wig. "That wig," he said, "has been worn by me for twelve years, and my father for thirty-two years, and my grandfather for another thirty-plus years, and his father before him, and so on, all the way back to the early nineteenth century." In short, he said, after a day's work in court "my scalp smelled so bad that my wife said it smelled like a dead horse." She cured the problem by sewing that linen hanky inside the wig. We all laughed. Funny story.

However, I took a lot more from that story than the other barristers. I was stunned by the heritage of that one wig and its connection to Victor's family. That wig was a treasured family heirloom sitting on the top of his head! What history English barristers have! Over so many centuries, despite Shakespeare's tome, English barristers have become legendary, mythic with a respect few professions can claim.

I often think that American lawyers have far too much incentive to win at all costs since winning translates into money. Barristers are amazed that American lawyers can talk juries into awarding so much money in damages, be it compensatory or punitive damages in personal injury cases. I was told that such awards cannot and do not happen in Britain. I was told that juries can only be had in certain limited cases such as defamation, fraud, false imprisonment, and malicious prosecution. Personal injury matters are tried by the Court and not juries. Thus, juries have no opportunity to run away with excessive damages awards simply because such juries do not exist. Less than 1% of civil trials are by juries. They do not have juries awarding 3 million dollars to a plaintiff who had hot coffee spilled in her lap, or a 4.9 billion dollar verdict against General Motors because GM, like all other car companies, put their fuel tanks in the rear, and the driver, with a BAL of two-and-a half times the legal limit of alcohol, crashed into the rear of another auto, when the car burst into flames.

When the public hear about these verdicts, they wonder about individual responsibility. I mean, we all know coffee in restaurants is served hot. We all know when you drive with a BAL that high, you may cause a horrific accident, no matter where the fuel tank is located. I do not mean to say that these plaintiffs or most any plaintiff does not have a viable cause of action against any such defendant, natural person or corporate. Corporations, like individuals, sometimes take short cuts to preserve the bottom line. These corporate decisions, by these legal actions, are made public, and all such companies that put products on the market should be safe to use. But what barristers have told me is that it becomes a game by lawyers for lawyers since all such cases are taken on a contingency basis and are seen as an opportunity for wealth by lawyers. That is why lawyers are said to be "bottom feeders," or that sharks won't attack lawyers because of "professional courtesy." The public perception is fueled by these cases, and we all know perception is reality. One barrister I spoke to was quite envious of me only because of my opportunity to make a great deal of money in a civil trial. I asked them about lawyer jokes. They laughed and said that such jokes are "reserved for American lawyers."

There is one criticism of American Criminal justice I hear all the time and that is there are thousands of people in prisons for mere possession and use of marijuana. I have never seen that to be the case. I have handled probably hundreds of drug possession cases and they rarely spend more than a day or two behind bars, whether it be California

170

or Wyoming. As is usually the case, since it is in most cases, a misdemeanor, they are put on probation for six months or given a deferment with no criminal record so long as they stay clean and do not break probation. Selling and delivering drugs is altogether a different situation. It is far more serious. In fact, it is a felony. Courts get rather serious with these offenders. You will spend some time in custody. Still, in most drug use cases they are placed on probation with suspended sentences. I have had numerous clients who have broken probation in as much as four times by using drugs again and still the court places them on probation, and some with insistence on some sort of outpatient or inpatient treatment. Prisons filled with simple drug users is not true. I have never seen it.

These repeat offenders sometimes graduate to being dealers and sellers and sometimes in their "business" commit violent offenses. Then we get into serious felony territory. But simple drug use, are the kind of offenses that the courts have long since become quite understanding in that they would rather the defendant pursue treatment rather than clog the jails, as the California Court did in the Drug Dad case in Chapter Fifteen above. When I hear TV new pundits tell of thousands in prisons over mere drug use, my heartburn starts to kick up. It simply is not true. If they are in prisons, there is far more to the story than is being reported.

To give an example, I had a case just recently in which the State was asking for two years of state prison for my client, one year to serve, one year suspended. What did my client do? He was lawfully stopped by an officer, and it was found that he had marijuana residue on his person. Residue! One would think that the system wishes to put my client in prison for merely having marijuana residue on his person! The media would have loved to go haywire over this case because of the State's insistence on prison time for possessing a tiny bit of grass! But that is not the whole story. My client had at least five prior offenses of drug possession, sales, delivery, and one violent felony burglary in his past. That's quite a record. Such prior offenses, it could be argued, demand some prison time. Our firm, as many firms would do, argued that a simple possession of marijuana residue does not translate into prison time. This is a valid argument, since over the past eleven years the client has led a clean life and the violent felony was nearly twenty years ago. We argued that remoteness in time as to the prior offenses and the mere possession charge should not require a prison sentence. Sure enough, the Court agreed and would not sentence the man to prison. The client was sentenced to 18 months state prison, but all suspended under the condition that he continue with out-patient drug treatment. Even if my client falls off the wagon, the court will most probably place him back on probation to try again. I have seen this many, many times.

Some states and communities are instituting "restorative justice" programs in schools. This involves getting the victim, the offender, and the community together to discuss their "feelings" regarding the crime. First, I have never known a victim of a crime would ever want to even be in the same room with any offender I have represented, let alone discuss his or her feelings with them. The victims tell me that they would be intimidated and victimized yet again by this arrangement. Then again, victim participation is completely voluntary as is the defendant. I have been told by a judge I respect that properly conducted, this type of an encounter can be transformative for both sides and help both move on. I admit, I have no experience with it. In Wyoming, restorative justice is time in a jail cell. Most victims I have seen believe that the offender never seems to get punished. In fact, offenders love the arrangement since they would say anything to prevent incarceration or punishment of any kind. Offenders I have known in my career never gave a damn about the "feelings" of any of their victims. The entire restorative justice system seems far too touchy/feely for me. Putting the justice system in the hands of social workers is a recipe for disaster. Coming from Brooklyn. I know all about bad people. It would never have worked in my neighborhood. It may work for some people, but not for a great many others. And that is the problem. In my practice, offenders need to know what they did, and how they did it, and to whom they did it will cause them to be incarcerated, that is, punished big time. I often-times tell sentencing judges that my client needs a lecture and a warning that if he sees them again, it's curtains. The client during the lecture gets bug-eyed, and sweats. It usually works. I do not believe "restorative justice" works with defendants with a 10-page rap sheet. The system would have to be quite selective on who participates in this program. To my mind it would be a good first-time offender program, nothing more.

Is the criminal justice system racist? I have no stories I could tell that would show there is institutional or systemic racism in the criminal justice system, in either California or Wyoming. Contrary to what you may hear in the media or what certain political action groups say or do, I personally have never seen an instance of institutional or systemic racism. In fact, I am offended by these charges of racism from politicians and young people who are far more interested in virtue signaling, than investigating the facts. They suggest that we, as lawyers, are part of that racism, and have never blown the whistle on any such conduct. Despite those political talking points by politicians who know absolutely nothing about the system, have never been knee deep in it, and simply wish to create as much friction as they can between groups for their own benefit, I have not seen this racism they speak of. In all my years in the system in California or Wyoming, I have not found race to be a factor in any case I was involved in. I have represented all kinds of people, White, Black, Native American, oriental, men, women, young, and old, straight, and gay. All the clients I had who were convicted of a crime had been so based on the elements of the crime charged and the evidence presented and sentenced based on the mitigating and aggravating factors. The law and the criminal statutes are detailed and specific and do not distinguish between races or any other groups.

As for sentencing, some minorities I have represented were treated lightly. I have never experienced a judge or a prosecutor who even appeared to use race, ethnic origin, etc. as a factor. The sentencing guidelines are clear. The issues of seriousness of the crime, the defendant's past criminal history, mitigating and aggravating circumstances, are all indications of the defendant's propensity to commit a crime. Even though I have had clients with past criminal convictions, I have had very few who were sent to prison whether it was a violent felony or whatever. I can only remember five clients in 40-plus years sent to prison, and none of them were minorities. The rest of the convictions resulted in some local time or probation. I have always believed that a thorough sentencing hearing with expert and lay witness testimony is the most productive way to prevent prison time. Accepting responsibility for one's misdeeds also helps quite a bit. Ask the good doctor in Chapter 25. In my career, sentencing hearings and the extensive presentation of mitigating factors have become an art form, and where a good lawyer can really show his stuff and earn his fee. I have found that many sentencing judges are loathed to send anyone to prison, no matter who they are. It is something they just do not want to do, or even look forward to doing. Just give a judge a good reason to not send a defendant to prison and you will succeed.

Court procedural rules and statutes that protect defendants are exhaustive. These rules and statutes range from traffic citations and misdemeanor and felony pleadings to rules governing media access to courts, selecting juries without bias, to rules of evidence as to what can be admitted into courts to prove guilt beyond a reasonable doubt. There are just too many court rules, and statutes that protect all defendants. And believe me, we defense attorneys have become quite creative in using these provisions to our advantage.

To give you an example, when I was in London watching a rape trial, the barristers were not permitted to ask any questions to any prospective jurors regarding any bias he or she may have as to the defendant, or the crime charged. It was "His Lordship" that asked if the juror could be fair and impartial. If the person said "yes," that was it. You're on the jury. The defense could challenge for cause, but on what basis? It must be that the juror was reasonably suspected of bias. Without vetting I do not know how that can be done. Here in America, we can ask many questions directly as to any potential bias the potential juror may have. We have numerous peremptory and unlimited challenges for cause. When I asked a barrister whether he felt comfortable with a vetting of only a few minutes by the judge and his not being able to ask any prospective juror any questions regarding a potential bias, his remark was, "primitive system, isn't it."

There has been a great discussion regarding "police brutality" and/or misconduct by the police. I must confess I have never seen it in any of my cases, both in California and Wyoming, except as described in chapter 5, by an over enthusiastic officer. In my experience if there is any violence by the police to an alleged offender it is usually because the individual resists arrest, refuses to cooperate, or cooperates in any way with the officer. When a person resists arrest and becomes violent all bets are off. Have never seen an officer go out of his way to injure or harm any potential defendant. Perhaps other lawyers have a different story. However, I must tell it like it is from my perspective, from what I have seen and experienced. As a footnote, we have 600,000 law enforcement officers in these United States, and only about a dozen incidences of brutality.

Be very skeptical of any political groups that yell "racism" or "social justice." They usually have a completely different agenda and use the race card as a means to create as much dissension as they can for their own political ends and goals. If there is systemic racism in this country, it is in the public educational system that refuses school choice to minorities. Sure, the wealthy send their kids to private or parochial schools and wouldn't be caught dead with their kids in a non-performing, underachieving public school. The "do-gooders" refuse to send disadvantaged kids to these private schools via vouchers, or charter schools! Never listen to what they say. Instead, look at what they do, and who they associate with, and who, if, they help. That will always determine who they really are. With a good quality education, we would have fewer need to send anyone to prison.

Women and the law have come into their own. When I was in law school in the seventies, we had about 80 students in my first year with only about a dozen women. Now I am being told the women outnumber the men in law school. I remember my first-year contracts professor would just torment these women during lecture and would go out of his way to pick them to recite a legal case, its facts, determination, and reasoning. He would ask them questions designed to embarrass them or "toughen" them up. He even stated that the test of a true women is "eggs over easy." At the end of the first year, these women gave him a gift, a large bronze pig with the inscription, "male chauvinist pig award for 1977." When he accepted the gift, he stated: "on behalf of my wife and four daughters, I thank you." The class roared with laughter.

Look, I have never had many problems with women lawyers. They are just as good and as bad as any male lawyer, and the new ones are just as stupid as young male lawyers. The problem I have had is the deliberate, if not, artificial, elevation of women to the bench. Talk about affirmative action. Politicians are so anxious to virtue signal and pander that they go overboard with their appointments to the bench. I can give two examples. In one case, I knew a lawyer who was a very good lawyer but had never tried a case in her career. She was chosen to be a Superior Court judge and shortly thereafter was chosen to be on the Court of Appeals! No fault as to her expertise. She was an excellent lawyer, but I believe the pendulum has swung in the opposite direction. With another, even inexplicable example, a legal secretary decided to go to law school and be a lawyer. Within only 13 years of her going to law school and after she had received her Bar license, she had been elevated to the Superior Court bench! Excuse me? I knew many lawyers, with far more experience, who coveted that judicial position. Perhaps in the future we will all be recognized by our qualifications only, and not by gender, race, sexual preference, etc. But don't count on it happening any time soon. I was always impressed by a quote from Vanessa Williams: "I knew they were going to make a big deal of my being Black, but I wish they'd ask me about my dancing." As for me, I was neither that crazy nor as ambitious as others. It's a tough job. I have always known my place in the world. Remember Dirty Harry, "a man has got to know his limitations."

My only concern as to some of you women lawyers is that sometimes you will over-compensate and be so uncooperative as to be quarrelsome. Not to say men are not as objectionable, but it is more difficult for us older lawyers to deal with. To all women lawyers: hey you're all terrific, take it easy on us old guys!

Lawyers and combat veterans. We live in a time where there are many thousands of combat veterans who have been embroiled in several wars in not only Vietnam, but Afghanistan, Iraq, Syria, Africa, etc. The VA hospitals are filled with them. They have seen the mouth of hell. As described in Chapter 11 and 16, Post traumatic Stress Disorder has been recognized by the courts as a mitigating factor to consider in all state and federal courts. When I started to practice law in 1981 it wasn't always that way. We young lawyers fought tooth and nail to convince the courts to recognize these combat veterans for the sacrifices they made for their country. Some of us were chastised and publicly humiliated by the press and members of the legal profession. Trust me on that. We lawyers tried to get the system to recognize that a high degree of combat exposure that occurs at a high operational tempo can cause numerous difficulties with transitioning to civilian life. These "addictive combat attachment" behaviors can be seen in many symptoms such as insomnia, addiction to adrenalin, re-experiencing the intense adrenalin rush, or "chasing the dragon," risky behaviors and sensation seeking, drug and alcohol addiction, re-experiencing traumatic events at a moment's notice, etc. The suicide rate among veterans is alarming! These veterans were taught to kill and survive. Once you have been through intense combat, for some, it's hard to put it all back in the box.

Many states now have Veterans Treatment Courts that divert these veterans away from the criminal justice system to emphasize treatment rather than punishment. In my "senior years" I have decided to put much of my expertise in representing these veterans. Currently, most of my cases are devoted to representing these combat veterans and to help them overcome the legal entanglements they find themselves in. Over the years it has become a specialty.

As advice, if you represent one of these fellows, get yourself the best psychologist that can be afforded. Worth their weight in gold. But do it quickly at the inception of the case. Do it before the state has a chance to secure the same expert. In my experience these experts are taken quite seriously by the courts. Once you have retained these experts, many of us keep their names in our contacts and use them in subsequent cases. You will develop a great working relationship with these doctors.

Finally, become familiar with the Veterans Administration. They can be a big help once you get through the bureaucracy. The VA can be penetrated. They will help if asked. But be patient. They are never quick to respond. There are many in-patient hospitals that specialize in PTSD, and their treatments such as cognitive behavioral therapy. It is far better to have your client in a VA hospital for inpatient care than in a county jail or state prison!

When representing a combat veteran in a criminal case the irony does not escape me. You have a client who is a combat veteran charged in the criminal justice system. He was once willing to sacrifice his life and do violence to protect our nation and our system of government. He now faces a different kind of violence in the form of incarceration, at the hands of the same government. A compelling argument is made that the government through the prosecution, the courts, the juries, and the justice system is also culpable in the matter. As in most of these cases, your client led a peaceful, stress-free, happy life prior to his time in combat. Life was good. These combat soldiers are all volunteers who serve because they love it. They serve because they love their country. It was not until their first combat tour, which they serve, "...at the request and for the convenience of the government," that the problems they now face began. Never met a soldier, sailor or Marine who balked at being sent to an "imminent danger pay area." It was for love of country.

It was the wars our nation became embroiled in, and the military training and indoctrination that created the source of the criminality: the client was trained to kill our enemies and survive. That is what they do. But that training and service had, for some, a terrible price, the veteran client's service-related disorders. I cannot and will not say that the nation or the State that is prosecuting my client, through its courts, has

179

done anything wrong. To the contrary. As much as I love my country, its military and the veterans and active-duty service members who serve, it is now time when all of us citizens accept our responsibility to those who have served us so well, to their own detriment. These veterans are deserving of much consideration in the form of rehabilitation and not incarceration.

What do you do with a dumb client who insists on not taking your sage advice? Good question. Here you are. You have spent four years in pre-law in college, three years in law school, you received your doctorate in law, spent a year or so with other lawyers to learn the ropes. You have been in the profession for a long time, you know how it works, you know how it does not work, you can even predict what a court will do in any given situation. Still, your client will not take your advice. Older lawyers resent this kind of client. Old, jaded lawyers will not tolerate a client who will not take their advice. There is no cure for stupidity. Sometimes it's incurable and could be fatal. I try not to worry about that much anymore. I just give them my best advice and let it go.

I have had many dumb clients. More than I can count. What is a dumb client? A dumb client calls you from the county jail and tells you he got busted yet again by the same officer for drug possession and being under the influence and tells you that "all I did was not make a complete stop at the stop sign!" A dumb client is an angry client who insists on making a statement to the court at sentencing. It never turns out well. A dumb client is a man who impregnated his fourth yet another woman out of wedlock and is again hit with child support. A dumb client is a man who signs a marital settlement agreement without reading it, and without benefit of counsel, and finds he has no visitation rights of his child. A dumb client is a man who has been in and out of prison and jail for 20 of the past 30 years and still has not realized that he is a lousy criminal and needs to move on to a different career.

A dumb client is a person who was stopped by an officer for a mere traffic ticket and proceeds to tell the officer he has meth in his glove compartment. A dumb client is someone who has a warrant for his arrest and insists on resisting when confronted by the police. It rarely turns out well and is the closest thing to attempted suicide, especially if the defendant has any kind of weapon on his person. A dumb client is one that no matter what you do for him, no matter how successful you are in his narrow escape from jail or state prison, is not happy with you because of the court's insistence on supervised probation. Most of all, a dumb client is a client who will not stop talking after any bust. It all reminds me of what John Wayne once said: "life can be hard. It's even harder when you're stupid."

Lawyers and alcohol. It is no secret that lawyers have the highest rates of alcohol abuse, according to the ABA. Nearly twenty percent, notably higher than the fifteen percent of surgeons who were abusing alcohol. Serious stress is the origin of the problem. The pressures a lawyer can face can be overwhelming. Preparing for a jury trial, the "magic" of preparing the right words to say to sway a jury, can be daunting. Next to lawyers and narcissism, I cannot think of a more damaging combination than lawyers who drink too much. All too often I have seen plenty of it. A couple of times, even in myself. Lawyers are a closed, often exclusive community of professionals. Once you have been seen in public in an intoxicated condition, people will talk. It will do harm to your reputation. And that will translate into lost clients and income. Alcoholism is bad enough in itself. When it is partnered with a court room lawyer it can be devastating, both for the lawyer and the client.

Let me give an example. In California, we all knew of this lawyer and his penchant for alcohol. We have seen him in an intoxicated condition far too often, even in courtrooms. The problem has been that we lawyers protected him far too often and had a blind eye to the problem. Very few said anything to help correct the behavior. On law and motion day, I was in the courtroom waiting for my case to be called and noticed that this lawyer was sitting at the Defendant's table listening to the Deputy DA's argument. He was to make his argument to the court momentarily. Suddenly, he quickly stood up, and in a slurred almost incomprehensible manner, asked to leave the court to go to the men's room. While standing, he urinated in his pants! It was obvious to everyone in the court. The judge was disgusted and began to castigate the man and asked the bailiff to escort him out of the courtroom. This was not the first incident but was the end of the line for this lawyer. He was suspended from the practice of law. Obviously, the State Bar had enough of this conduct. His practice had suffered mightily in the past, but this was too much. I'm sure the client he was representing that day was not a happy man. For such lawyers, it's a long, hard road to getting back in the good graces of the State Bar, and in the legal community.

Lawyers who regularly abuse alcohol have a best friend in their State Bar and their local county Bar Association. These associations will go out of their way to help lawyers with this most prevalent problem. They will refer you to alcohol abuse counselors, centers, even assign mentors from the Bar to help with the problem. I have known county judges who watch over their "flock" of lawyers like pastors at a church meeting. The help is there.

Is the justice system perfect? Of course not. The justice system has never declared such, or even pretends to be. Insofar as my experiences with the system, I can only give you my perspective from two truly diverse states, California, and Wyoming. These two states could not be more different. California is very cosmopolitan, quite liberal in its social and political attitudes, and has a huge budget of $215 billion, with even greater spending habits, with a population of over 37 million, and with a population of over 253 people per square mile.

Wyoming, in contrast, is very conservative, politically, and socially, and has a much smaller budget of only $9 billion, with a population of just under 600,000. There are more people in the Sacramento area than in the entire state of Wyoming! The state has a population density of less than 6 people per square mile. Wyoming is a very rural state. Metropolitan areas in Wyoming are really non-existent. You can drive several hours and not see a single person. Its "cities" each have a population in the thousands if not hundreds, not millions as in California. The people in the cowboy state live a different kind of existence than you would find in California or most other states for that matter. Life is a bit harder, a bit more challenging. Ranch work is tougher, the winters are colder and can be inconvenient.

The cultural divide is even greater. Of course, metropolitan areas in California will have a much higher rate of crime per 100,000 people than non-metropolitan areas in Wyoming. For example, in 2011, there was a total of 5,086 bank robberies reported, with only 2 percent of those happening in rural areas. [FBI Bank Crime Statistics Wash. DC; U.S. Department of Justice, 2012] So, of course, when coupled with each State's social and political values, a different approach by each legal system can be seen, but not as much as you would think. California judges are always reluctant to jail defendants and always look for a different approach if it can be done, especially in drug offenses. Wyoming judges are not much different, they do the same. I have found no real difference in either state's approach to sentencing. However, California may have changed since I left. The same approach can be seen in violent offenses in both states. Both are intolerant of people hurting other people. You will spend some time in jail.

However, change is coming. As of the writing of this book, crime is way up in all categories from misdemeanors to felonies. You would think in the twenty-first century, we have figured out what works and what does not. But we have not. New age district attorneys have, in effect, become public defenders. Protecting the public is no longer job one. Felonies have become misdemeanors and misdemeanors have become...well you know the story. Did any of us ever think a person would be able to casually walk into a department store and steal anything they can get their hands on without as much as a reproach? In some states a real difference that can be seen is the new approach by California and New York as to bail. Cashless bail has become the new thing with the left and will die on that podium. I cannot see Wyoming in the foreseeable future permitting any accused offender to be released without bail, or casually stealing big ticket items without being confronted big time. Protecting the public is upper-most in their minds, both by the authorities, and by the general public. The same can also be said of the Court's attitude toward career criminals with numerous prior offenses. Get the number of that bail bondsman. Wyoming has no patience with those defendants. Some are fighting back with this insanity. And yet, some are crazy. For example, recently the Illinois Supreme Court ruled the governor's feel-good no cash bail system has been ruled as constitutional. For the defenseless in Illinois, there is little hope out there. I fear that if the government does not do its job and protect the public, the public may do it for them. Self-preservation is always alive and well. It is human nature. Again, without a thorough and detailed risk assessment of the defendant and repeat offenders the public is in danger of human predators.

Another difference is the contrast between the two states as to personal self-defense. In Wyoming, anyone entering your home without permission with the apparent intent to do harm takes his life in his hands. I know of no state that has more guns per capita and more willingness to use them than Wyoming. Owning many guns and thousands of rounds of ammunition are commonplace. Guns are carried by many, either openly or concealed since no permit is required. Wyomingites are believers in personal responsibility for the safety of your home and loved ones. They are truly the "first responders," not the local police or Sheriff's Department. The deputies here in Wyoming seem to have more common sense in that regard. In fact, any stranger who enters another person's home unlawfully is presumed to be doing so with criminal intent involving force and violence. A person who is attacked in any place he has a right to be, has no apparent duty to retreat before using any reasonable defensive force, even if they had an opportunity to retreat. Wyoming is a stand your ground state. Self-defense is believed to be the most basic of rights. God help any person or group of people who threaten a person's family, home, and hearth.

In contrast, California is not a stand your ground state, and no statute specifically gives you that right. You may have an affirmative duty to retreat even from a place you have a right to be if you were confronted with a first strike. It all depends on the circumstances. Some lawyers I know argue you do have the right to use force without first trying to escape. It all seems rather vague and gives too many jurors an opportunity for virtue signaling to convict a defendant who was confronted with a situation (or an "opportunity") to use a firearm to defend himself or his family. I like Wyoming's self-defense laws; they are more specific and give self-defense the respect it deserves.

The biggest difference in the two states is in the makeup of the juries. Juries in California, especially in the metropolitan areas, are far easier to manipulate and are more amenable to be given a crying towel. I have found California jurors to be wealthier, more liberal, more diverse, and more apt to be guilt ridden over a defendant as also being a "victim." You could never do that in Wyoming. Their jurors make up what I consider "law-and-order juries," who do not tolerate the excuses of people who allegedly do bad things. As a negative, I have even felt that you must prove the defendant innocent rather than the State proving the defendant guilty beyond a reasonable doubt. Other defense lawyers have expressed the same belief. Not a good situation. The same hard juries can also be found in the more rural counties of California and are more similar in beliefs and values to Wyoming juries than they are to the juries in the metropolitan areas. California is diverse.

With jury makeup, you try to prevent bias. However, there is just so much you can do in jury voir dire. You cannot look inside their heads and know what they are thinking. When questioned, they will tell you they are fair and impartial, but you know, despite all your enlightened directions in your closing argument, many will either forget or toss away that jury instruction for reasonable doubt and go with their impulse to find guilt. Most trial lawyers know that certain groups as jurors will be more advantageous than others. In a criminal trial you do not want anyone who has a relative or friend as a police officer. Military people are sticklers to rules and regulations and not very sympathetic. Older jurors are more sympathetic to young witnesses. That sort of thing. We have a hell of a list of perfect juror types. But as Lillian Hellman once said: "Nobody outside of a baby carriage or a judge's chamber believes in an unprejudiced point of view."

Let me give you an anecdote. In California, during a jury voir dire, I asked a prospective juror if he believed all policemen told the truth. The man looked at me and just let go. He began telling the court that not only do police lie on a regular basis, but that they once tried to accuse him of committing some crime. He went on and on, his voice increasing in volume and excitable, telling the court what this officer had done, that he never committed a crime, and would never trust a policeman on anything again. After he was through, I stood up and said to the court: " Mr.---- is acceptable to the defense, your honor." The entire court was drowned in laughter! Of course, the prosecutor challenged the man for cause.

Because of the expected makeup of hard juries in Wyoming, you just do not go to trial unless you believe in your client's innocence, the facts and evidence are in your favor, and the client wants to take the matter to trial. The decision to go to trial is always up to the client, never the lawyer. All you could do is give them your best advice and hope it all works out.

All in all, the system may not be perfect, but it generally works. Sure, we lawyers hear about all kinds of stories of justice denied. We hear about the rapist who walks away without punishment; the man who shoots a 30-year-old woman in San Francisco and is found not guilty; the woman who's 2-year-old child disappeared and who didn't report her missing for a month, but instead went to night clubs, had a spending spree, got a tattoo, and yet was found not guilty. Sure, we all hear about these cases. Is this the fault of the system or the jurors who refused to convict? If it is the jurors who refused to weigh the evidence, what does it say about our culture? I find it difficult to comment on these cases since I was not there and have no first-hand information on how these cases developed.

If the purpose of the justice system is to preserve peace and order in the culture, then I would say it does a fair job. We do not have widespread vigilante justice anymore (thus far). Movies such as 'Death Wish' and 'The Equalizer' are just that, movies. But the popularity of these movies may be a signal that we are going in the wrong direction. Sometimes we are overwhelmed. The system does punish evil doers, not perfectly, but it does punish. Many people believe the system does not punish criminals as it should and in effect does not protect the innocent from the bad guys. These people have a good point since a defendant being placed back on the street after being arrested for throwing an old lady off the train platform, or beating a man near to death, does not instill confidence in the system. The courts can only do what the laws (and the politicians) tell them they can do. Hence the frustration we in the system experience. It greatly depends on the laws and the prosecutors of the state you live in. However, it does establish relative justice and relative tranquility. It does try to rehabilitate wrongdoers, and from what I have seen, to a fault. Would anyone rather have justice be dispensed pursuant to the system in The People's Republic of China where defendants just disappear? I don't think so.

I can only comment on my own experiences with the system. I can tell you with confidence that the people I have known within the system are good people doing a thankless job. The people in the system go out of their way to make sure that all who find themselves in it are treated fairly. I have nothing but admiration, respect and love for the court clerks, bailiffs, shorthand reporters, judicial assistants, and all who have a hand in making it all work. These are the people who make it all happen. They make it all work. Risking repetition, in many respects these good people are the real power in the courts. To all new lawyers, make friends with these people. They will save your butt more than can be counted. I know this to be true.

Why retire? We all know when it is time. It is time when you forget simple legal phrases in oral argument. It is time when you forget the name of the opposing counsel you have appeared with for years. It is time when you supplement your diet with MCT oil powder and coconut oil for memory. It is time when your wife says: "Enough is enough." It is time when you cringe when the phone rings. It is more than time when you say: "should I answer that?"

For many of us being a lawyer is not just a job or even a career choice. It has become an identity, that "life choice." The question becomes, can you live without that identity? Some of us never try to retire and continue until death. Those individuals have become so identified with their "life choice" that to strip them of that identity would leave them with nothing significant in its place. I have seen it many times. I know lawyers who were still practicing in their nineties, their offices still open! With some lawyers, the identity they have cultivated can be so pervasive that to lose it, they become lost and unable to cope. That can be dangerous and not a formula for a happy time in your 'golden years.' On the other hand, some of us do retire, hang up that Armani, or in my case, that Macy's suit and place it in a forgotten suit bag. I feel luckier than most. I would rather sip a banana daiquiri on my boat or saddle up, than try to rearrange a person's life for him or her to see the light. I paid my dues and then some. I also have other interests. I am a fair finish carpenter and furniture maker. I raise horses and love my trips with my wife in the back country. I still have those drums I purchased back in the sixties and used professionally. Who knows, my life may come full circle!

You may ask? Ok, you are retired. But are you still a due's paying active member of the Bar? What a foolish question to ask. Of course, I am! You never know what may come up!